Local Power in the Japanese State

Local Power in the Japanese State

Muramatsu Michio

Translated by Betsey Scheiner
and James White

UNIVERSITY OF CALIFORNIA PRESS

Berkeley / Los Angeles / London

Originally published as *Chihō jichi*,
© 1988 Daigaku Shuppankai

University of California Press
Berkeley and Los Angeles, California

University of California Press, Ltd.
London, England

© 1997 by
The Regents of the University of California

Library of Congress Cataloging-in-Publication Data

Muramatsu, Michio, 1940–
    [Chihō jichi. English]
    Local power in the Japanese state / Muramatsu Michio ; translated
by Betsey Scheiner and James White.
        p.   cm.
    Includes bibliographic references and index.
    ISBN 0-520-07275-8 (cloth : alk. paper).—ISBN
0-520-07276-6 (pbk. : alk. paper)
    1. Local government—Japan.   2. Central-local government
relations—Japan.   3. Local government.   4. Central-local
government relations.   I. Title.   II. Series.
JS7373.A2   1997
320.8'0952'09045—dc 20   96-41515
                                                              CIP

9 8 7 6 5 4 3 2 1

The publisher gratefully acknowledges the funding by the Sasakawa
Peace Foundation and the Pacific Basin Institute in support of this
translation.

Contents

Illustrations

Figures

Tables

Preface to English Edition

The original, Japanese edition of this book was published in 1988. A few years later, in 1993, the rule of the Liberal Democratic Party (LDP), which had been in power since its creation in 1955, came to an end. Japan entered a period of political turmoil, in which it became extremely difficult to predict which party would hold power. Some background on this turmoil is important for understanding the passage of new measures affecting local government in 1995.

The fall of the LDP led to the birth of the administration of Morihiro Hosokawa, an epoch-making event in Japanese politics. Hosokawa's power base included the Socialist Party and Komeitō (Clean Government Party), as well as the newly organized Nihon Shintō (Japan New Party), Sakigake Party, and Shinseitō (Renewal Party), which had broken off from the LDP. Underlying this political change was the public's increasing tolerance of the Socialist Party, owing to the end of the cold war, and also its growing discontent with the LDP. LDP governments had long favored rural interests while neglecting the interests of urban consumers, and the public's dissatisfaction resembled a time bomb, which finally exploded in the wake of numerous scandals involving party finance.

Party reorganization had only started when the Hosokawa administration took office. Centrist elements supporting the cabinet consolidated into the New Frontier Party (Shinshintō), but their coalition with the Socialists was to be short-lived. The two sides took opposing stances on basic issues, including constitutional reform. Prime Minister Tsutomu Hata's New Frontier Party administration, which followed the

Hosokawa administration, collapsed when the Socialists left the ruling coalition. The LDP then joined forces with the Socialists and the Saki- gake Party, and together they created a cabinet under Socialist Party chairman Tomiichi Murayama. The Socialists steadily retreated from their earlier policy positions during their participation in the coalition government. For example, they withdrew their long-standing opposi- tion to the U.S.-Japan Security Treaty system and moderated their posi- tion on Article 9 (the antiwar clause) of the constitution. The issues fac- ing Japanese politicians during the Murayama administration were a faltering economy, the damage caused by the great Hanshin earthquake, social unease following the terrorist violence of the AUM Shinrikyō re- ligious sect, and the problem of bad loans due to unsound investments in real estate during the so-called economic bubble. In other words, there were few cheerful issues. The public, which finally became unhappy with the Murayama administration's incompetence, began to seek the LDP's return to power, even though the LDP itself had recently been severely criticized by the public.

Prime Minister Murayama finally resigned in January 1996. The coali- tion government of the LDP and the Socialists continued, but it was now led by LDP politician Ryutaro Hashimoto. The public waited anx- iously to see whether this would be the first stage of a new period of LDP rule or if Japan would utilize its experience of the past few years to develop a system permitting the genuine alternation of parties in office. The coalition government of the LDP and the Socialists is relevant to the research contained in this book because the Diet passed, in May 1995, the Law to Promote Decentralization (referred to here as the Decentraliza- tion Law). This crucial law could affect local governments and their rela- tionship to the central government, and it probably would not have passed if the LDP's one-party rule had continued. By the fall of 1996, two midterm reports related to the law had been published. Their contents include proposals for radical decentralization.

The debate regarding local government reforms, which led to the De- centralization Law, began when local government issues were placed on the agenda of administrative reform in the early 1980s. The Second Pro- visional Administrative Reform Commission (Daini Rinchō) was an advisory committee formed to make proposals on administrative re- form. Its orientation was neo-liberal, and it was supposed to enact the Japanese counterpart to the administrative reforms carried out by Prime Minister Margaret Thatcher in Great Britain and President Ronald Rea- gan in the United States. Yasuhiro Nakasone and other reform-minded

LDP Diet members played key roles in the political process of Japan's administrative reforms.

The Daini Rinchō's reforms affected local governments in many ways: one reform, for example, reduced the conditional subsidies given by the central ministries to local governments. In addition, an important feature of the Daini Rinchō was that it provided a forum where politicians and bureaucrats from Tokyo and from the localities could debate issues concerning the central-local relationship. Although the Daini Rinchō's legal term of existence ended in 1983, problems involving local government continued to be a central concern of the First, Second, and Third Administrative Reform Promotion Commissions, all of which worked on administrative change. Of the four subcommittees of the third commission, one was specifically assigned to address local government systems. Hosokawa, who later became prime minister, was then the governor of Kumamoto prefecture, and he served as one of the leaders of this subcommittee.

The local government subcommittee proposed many governmental reforms, and in 1994, under the Hosokawa administration, these were approved at a cabinet meeting in a document entitled "Regarding the Policy of Promoting Future Administrative Reform." Based on this cabinet decision, a subcommittee on decentralization was created within the Administrative Reform Promotion Office, which itself was under the authority of the cabinet. Next, based on the proposals of the subcommittee on decentralization, the cabinet approved the "General Policy Regarding the Promotion of Decentralization" on December 25, 1994, and it prepared plans for promoting the decentralization of political authority. As mentioned above, the Decentralization Law was passed by the Diet in 1995, under the Murayama administration. Based on this law, the Decentralization Promotion Committee was attached to the prime minister's office, and it began holding sessions preparatory to the drafting of a new reform plan for decentralization.

Two conclusions may be drawn from all this. One is that the Decentralization Law is a product of the current period of political turmoil, which has continued since the breakdown of the LDP's long-standing one-party rule. The other is that decentralization is slowly but steadily being promoted. As expressed in Tip O'Neill's favorite phrase, "All politics is local politics," many interests are involved in the relationship between the central government and local electoral districts, and this means that the debate over local government reform can proceed only in increments.

The Decentralization Promotion Committee is supposed to produce a report within five years. Yet many people may question whether Japan's local governmental system, including central-local relations, will really change much as a result of the Decentralization Law. I believe that reforms will indeed be implemented. However, the reforms are likely only to mitigate, not eliminate, the type of central government involvement in local affairs referred to in this book as vertical administrative control. Furthermore, I think it probable that the local government pressures on the center, which I call horizontal, or lateral, political competition, will also persist. In other words, I believe that the models presented in this book will continue to be relevant despite the changes currently under way.

There are at least two reasons why decentralization is attracting so much attention in Japan today. The first is that Japan is currently undergoing a period of political transformation. During periods of transformation, local government systems tend to attract attention in Japan because local government is inevitably involved in any major administrative change. So much responsibility is already delegated to local governments that any administration reform must affect central-local relations. The structure of political confrontation, which consisted of political cleavages rooted in the cold war, has disappeared, and the main issue being contested now is whether to have a large or small government. The resolution of this issue will depend to a great extent on how the government handles the whole problem of decentralization.

The second reason decentralization is salient is that the volume of activity of Japan's local governments, as measured by their expenditures, is large. In the general account the expenditures of the Japanese government total roughly 110 billion yen (1.1 billion dollars), of which more than two-thirds is spent by local authorities. Proposals regarding the size of government or the level of government activity, both of which are measured largely in terms of expenditure, therefore have a direct impact on the issue of decentralization. Although decentralization reforms have been taken up repeatedly since World War II, all the earlier efforts, in the 1940s through the 1970s, were promoted by progressives and leftists. In contrast, the current effort reflects pressure from business and key economic groups to reduce the level of government activity. These groups stress "small government" and deregulation, and they see decentralization as one step toward the realization of a smaller government.

Reformers face the two challenges of easing regulations and reducing the level of government spending and activity. Realistically, what is likely to result from their efforts? One possibility (option A) is to carry out deregulation and reduce government activity simultaneously. This approach would curb central government regulations, loosen the control of local governments by the central government, and reduce the level of activity of both central and local governments. This sort of decentralization would be welcomed by business. Among the political parties, it is the ideal image of the state held by neo-liberals, who stand out among the leaders of the New Frontier Party. A second possibility (option B) is that the central government will deregulate and trim its size, while the activities of local governments will increase to even higher levels. This option could be said to entail the acceptance of a welfare "state" at the local level. Should these options both fail to be realized, the only other alternative (option C) is to maintain the current welfare state without reducing regulations or the level of government activity. This would be the choice of the left wing of the LDP and of the Social-Democratic Party (the former Japan Socialist Party). It would also please municipal governments and central government ministries and agencies. They like the status quo.

In my view, option A is probably not a viable option for Japan, where the average age of the population is increasing rapidly. As many people have predicted, government expenditures are bound to increase to cope with the aging population. Option B currently has the most vocal support. While its proponents would continuously implement deregulation at the center, they would be less likely to trim welfare activities. However, there is a strong possibility that the status quo (option C) will be maintained, and that no substantial change will occur.

Finally, I would like to address the relationship between the models I use in the text and the orthodox understanding of local governmental systems in advanced economies. Ordinarily, local government systems may be classified into two types: the separationist model, which is found in the United States and Great Britain, and the integrationist model, which is prominent in continental Europe. Japan's local government system is similar to the integrationist local government systems found on the European continent. Originally, in fact, Japan modeled its modern local governmental system after those of Prussia and France. It is interesting to note that in integrationist states, it is common for movements to form that try to move things closer to the types of local government found in the United States and Great Britain. Such was the case in France, for instance, where a decentralization law was passed in 1985.

Japan's centralized legal system prescribes an integrationist system of local government, combined with some elements of the separationist model bequeathed to it by the postwar U.S. occupation authorities. Many of Japan's academics would clearly prefer a separationist model of local government, and the Japanese debate on local autonomy has been led by a desire for greater decentralization. Consequently, much research has highlighted what I call the vertical administrative control model, emphasizing excessive central control over local governments. But I see the intense relationship between central and local governments as having sprung from local political initiatives as well. In my observation, the Japanese version of the integrationist model has evolved by means of a long-standing and two-sided process of political and administrative interaction between center and locality.

Japan's recently enacted Decentralization Law is a significant but still limited move in the direction of a separationist model of local government. As suggested earlier, I doubt whether the eventual scope of Japan's current reform project will prove all-encompassing. The country's system of local government is likely to remain within the general boundaries of the integrationist model.

I would like to take this opportunity to express my most sincere gratitude to Betsey Scheiner and James White, whose joint translation of this work is of the highest order. I would also like to thank Matthew Santamaria for his invaluable assistance during the last stage of editing.

12 November 1996

Preface to Original Edition

Theories of local government developed when the world was still composed of decentralized, agrarian societies. Yet advanced industrialization and the urbanization of society have not brought an end to local government; it has continued to survive, along with various other elements of the decentralized early modern state. Its focus, however, has had to adapt, since conditions have greatly changed. Rapid economic development has strengthened the interdependence of central and local governments, and today the central-local relationship has become close in every developed state. In addition, waves of influence from the international sphere have swept across regional society. And the present information age is beginning to raise a number of questions—for example, what kinds of principles should govern the interface between the computers of central ministries and of local governments? In the future, as the populations of industrial societies age, the welfare functions of local governments will expand and the frequency of intergovernmental cooperation will increase.

In times like ours, when central-local relations are intense, is the autonomy of local governments still significant? Is it even possible? The answer to both questions is "yes." But what does that mean in practical terms?

This book analyzes forty years of local government and central-local relations in postwar Japan. The first chapter provides a comparative perspective, touching on the broad realities and principles of central-local relations in advanced industrialized states. It also introduces Japanese debates over local government through the theories of two scholars of public administration (Nagahama Masatoshi and Tsuji Kiyoaki). Chapter 2 describes how these two theories have become orthodox and discusses their content. These theories, which suggest an absence of local autonomy, have dominated debate for a long time, although recently contradictory arguments have been presented in a number of places. A third, newer theory argues that the bottom-up political competition of local government in fact determines central-local relations. Chapter 3 attempts to explain this theory, based on an analysis of interviews with prefectural governors, since the popular election of governors was a major factor in the great postwar reform that transformed the role of the prefectures and encouraged local autonomy. Chapter 4 continues this effort, attempting to demonstrate the adequacy of the new model at the municipal level. In Chapter 5 I reinvestigate the concept of local government overall using the new perspective, and in Chapter 6 I provide an understanding of the nature of Japanese local government. As this book relates, *chihō jichi,* the common Japanese term for local government, connotes not just local autonomy but also "self-management" or "self-control." This kind of autonomy has been or can be achieved to a great extent even in highly centralized present-day Japan. But to observe and analyze it we must go beyond studies of control strategies of the center over local governments, lower the focus of our discussion to the municipal level, and analyze the process of local government operation. This book is based on a study of the government of the city of Kyoto (Miyake and Muramatsu 1981), but additional studies of government processes on the local level are needed to provide a comprehensive and conclusive analysis. I hope in the future to analyze further the structure and processes of local government.

It has taken a long time to write this book, and it has built upon the research of many other scholars, who deserve my deepest thanks. I especially enjoyed the intellectual stimulation of Nagahama Masatoshi's *Chihō jichi* (1952), which fostered my interest in local government, and the penetrating analysis of Japan's political administration by Tsuji Kiyoaki, whose views have served as the paradigm of orthodoxy in Japanese political science. Katō Kazuaki deepened my understanding of the present situation in local government. When I was in the midst of conceptualizing this book, Terry MacDougall and Ōmori Wataru organized a conference, where I was able to exchange ideas with scholars of central-local government relations in other countries. I was heartened to learn that a number of scholars overseas were advancing theories in the same direction as I. I especially profited from participating in conferences in Turin, Bellagio, and New York with Robert Putnam, Bruno Dente, Sidney Tarrow, Douglas Ashford, Michael Aiken, Peter Lang, and Richard Samuels. As for the data and research materials treated here, I would like to acknowledge with thanks the Gyōsei Kanri Kenkyū Sentā (1985) study and my colleagues there: Ōmori Wataru, Nakamura Akira, Takeshita Yuzuru, Kitahara Tetsuya, and Koike Osamu. I am also grateful to Yonehara Junshichirō for allowing me to use his data in chapter 5. I commissioned the Chūō Chōsasha to carry out the survey of governors. Many people lent a hand in preparing the data and manuscript for this book, and I am particularly indebted to Horibe Kiyoko and Kobayashi Yasushi for their help in the final stages.

Lastly, I would like to thank Inoguchi Takashi, who planned and promoted the Contemporary Japanese Politics series and gave me the opportunity to write this volume, and Takenaka Toshihide of the University of Tokyo Press, which published the series. Neither remote nor interfering, Mr. Takenaka took exactly the right stance to lead this book to completion.

This book is dedicated to my daughters, who sent their support to their often absent father.

26 March 1988

CHAPTER I

A Sketch of Postwar Local Government

A Comparative Perspective

JAPAN'S LOCAL GOVERNMENT SYSTEM: A GLOBAL PERSPECTIVE

This chapter asks whether, within whatever context, there are appropriate comparisons for Japanese local government and, if so, which issues should be considered. It then suggests a way to account for the special characteristics of intergovernmental relations in Japan.

In order to understand something about a country, to "know" it in a social scientific way, we must use a comparative perspective. In the case of Japanese local government, the first comparisons that come to mind are those with Prussia and France, which influenced the Meiji local government system, and with the U.S. local government system, which had an impact through the postwar Occupation reforms. But any consideration of contemporary central-local relations and local government in Japan should include not just the countries where the Japanese system has its roots but as many advanced capitalist nations with Western-style constitutions as possible. It is also desirable to consider the local governments of developing and socialist nations. From this broadened view, the local government systems of the world can be classified as follows:

1. Local government in unitary states (advanced industrial nations)
   a. Centralized
   b. Decentralized

2. Local government in federal systems (advanced industrial nations)
   a. Centralized
   b. Decentralized
3. Local government in socialist states
4. Local government in developing nations

Now, having listed all the possibilities, can we narrow the range of relevant countries in order to conduct a comparative analysis of local government in contemporary Japan? First, let us consider local government in the socialist states. Even supposing that these countries possessed a common ideology—and it is not clear that they do—the conduct of government operations varies greatly from country to country, and their local government systems are among their points of greatest difference. It is inappropriate to group the former Soviet Union, Cuba, and China together. More fundamentally, very little can be learned by placing their various socialist local governments, about which relatively little reliable information is available, in a comparative framework with Japanese local government.

Next, take local systems in the developing nations. There are a great many of them, and they vary tremendously in climate, physical attributes, historical development (especially the influence of former colonial states), and, above all, level of development. But research has only begun on individual countries, and—as with the socialist states—little information is available. Under present conditions, a systematic comparison to the local government systems of these countries would be difficult.

In contrast, for the advanced industrial countries with unitary or federal systems, a good deal of research on their local governments has been done and is relevant to theories of Japanese local government. The most useful comparisons are among local governments of advanced industrial nations with Western-style constitutions. In this light, using the schema of Iwasaki Mikiko (1985), I would like to locate the Japanese local system roughly within a worldwide framework for local governments.

Table 1 shows three types of decentralization presented by Iwasaki. The first, which characterizes federal systems, is "political decentralization." Its most important point is that the equality of the central structure and local governments is stipulated in the constitution. Its special features are a high degree of financial autonomy and the election of top local officials. The second type is "administrative decentralization." In

Table 1 *Three Types of Decentralization*

	Political Decentralization (Division of power between central authority and local governments not in hierarchical relationship to central authority)	Administrative Decentralization (Division of power between central authority and local governments in hierarchical relationship to central authority)	Deconcentration (Partial transfer of central authority's power to organs subordinate to central authority)
Legal foundation for local government's authority	Constitution	Central authority	Central authority
Relationship between local government and central authority	Equal	Occasional local subordination to central authority	Local organs completely subordinate to central authority
Financial support for local government	Financially independent[a]	Partial financial independence	Financially dependent on central authority
Position of local government	Independent of central authority	Created by central authority but partially autonomous	Local agency of central government
Method of selecting local government leader	Election	Election or appointment	Appointment

SOURCE: Iwasaki 1985: 28.

[a]André Lajoie (1968: 6) defines financial independence (*auto-financement*) as the ability to secure revenues to pay the costs of exercising one's jurisdiction.

this model, the legal basis for local government lies in the law—that is, in the central government. But even though local government is located in a framework that is necessarily dependent on the center, it is not completely dependent. It enjoys, at least partially, both financial and structural autonomy; its officials include some who are elected and some who are not. In the third model, "deconcentration," the local government administration is politically subordinate to the center as well as legally based on a delegation of authority from the center. Top officials are appointed by the state. As a result, local government is almost a branch office of the center. Not only does local government depend completely on the will of the center for its existence, it is financially dependent as well.

As a whole, these categories are valid, but they derive a little too much from legal theory, and their concept of politics is too limited. For example, on the basis of the definitions given above, it would seem that the ideal form of political decentralization has never existed in unitary states, but in fact a high degree of political decentralization can be seen in many unitary states. Therefore, it is important to ask how this type of local government, viewed as a political process, is established and under what conditions (including legal conditions). Certainly, systemic differences are of essential importance, whether simply in their function as rules of the game or as a part of the constitutional structure. Clearly, the power of the system must be evaluated first of all. But the extent to which a legal system can regulate local government or intergovernmental relations is limited, and thus the explanatory power of the legal system by itself is weak.

For example, the cases encompassed by the second category of table 1, administrative decentralization, run the gamut from some very decentralized systems to some that resemble the branch-office model of the third category, with nothing to distinguish between them. Japan, for example, is a unitary state, but its local governments cannot be seen as merely branch offices—indeed, Japan falls into the second category. But when one tries to grasp the special quality of Japan's local government by comparing it to other countries, the categories in the table alone do not provide many insights. In order to compare the variations among cases of "administrative decentralization," we need a typology that takes elements other than legal systems—such as politics—into consideration.

Nevertheless, the three categories cited above do have a number of uses. One that Iwasaki did not predict is their usefulness in analyzing theories of political movements related to local government. Political decentralization has become a normative model for proponents of strong local government in administratively decentralized countries, *or the countries so perceived*. It is not that these proponents want unitary countries to become federal systems; rather, they idealize the decentralized type of local government frequently seen in federal countries (for example, the United States or Switzerland) and use it as a normative model to reform the system they have. In contrast, the deconcentration model, in which local government becomes a branch office, serves as a model of what they do not want.

As I have said, variations within the three categories are important—not only for the second type but for the first as well. Moreover, not only does the first category allow for the most autonomous local governments and the greatest diversity in the practice of central-local relations or intergovernmental relations; it also facilitates original conceptualizations of them. In the United States especially—where a federal system has, since the 1930s, attempted a variety of practices as political science has developed—a wealth of views has been generated. I have found these views useful in analyzing Japanese central-local relations, and I would thus like first to touch on the development of American theories of intergovernmental relations. I should note that legally, the United States and Japan contrast sharply. In the first case, we have a thoroughly decentralized country; in the second, a country with a centralized past, which many people consider even now to be centralized. Therefore, in comparing the two countries, we shall move initially toward the discovery of differences rather than commonalities. But by the last stages of our comparison, it is possible that we will also be able to appreciate strongly their commonalities as advanced industrial nations.

THE UNITED STATES AND JAPAN

First, for a long time American political scientists were concerned with local government independent of outside forces. Only relatively recently have intergovernmental relations drawn their attention (Martin 1965; Elazer 1965). American political scientists concerned with local government turned first to an analysis of local power structures. A vigorous debate developed between the view represented by Floyd Hunter (1953), who saw U.S. communities as having local power structures, and the pluralist view represented by Robert Dahl (1961). Interestingly, the participants in the debate over community power structures showed almost no concern for intergovernmental relations, because they assumed that the United States had a decentralized form of local government.

Conversely, in countries that are considered centralized, there is very little interest in community power structures. Japan is a case in point: studies of local government are almost entirely limited to intergovernmental relations. It seems to be assumed that the decentralized form of local government is impossible in Japan; therefore, there is no need to study local politics.

Second, there are different political implications in what is emphasized about local government. In the United States the emphasis on autonomy, or home rule, appears particularly in the suburbs of large cities. It is common knowledge that in the United States middle-class whites have fled from the heart of cities in response to an increase in the number of people of color (especially blacks) there. The population of municipalities on the outskirts of these cities has accordingly expanded. In California, for example, when people fled into unincorporated areas, new municipalities were soon created. When new local governments did not form, people took steps (as in the Lakewood plan in California) to purchase urban services from nearby local governments that assumed the role of a central city. In any case, the people who moved to the suburbs devised government procedures or social and economic arrangements (such as real estate distribution systems) to keep those different from themselves from entering. The best example of this is the case of exurbanites who set up their own local governments and used their legislative power to zone their municipalities for large minimum-lot sizes. Because the number of people who could afford to purchase large tracts of land was limited, this restricted new entries into the community. This method was also used to deal with enforced school busing for the racial integration of schools. In the suburbs, by maintaining the autonomy of school districts in communities where different social classes could not enter, people were able to make enforced busing substantively useless. The suburban local governments insisted that they were simply upholding the principle of home rule. Autonomy was clearly being used for a conservative purpose.

In contrast, an emphasis on decentralized local government in Japan is considered progressive, as making Japan more like the United States and Europe. The premise of this view is the perception that even after the war Japan was a bureaucratic, centralized state. Therefore, in order to oppose the centralized state, liberals and socialists had to cooperate in producing autonomy at the local level. From the outset, some liberals found in the labor unions a political base from which to oppose the state. Local autonomy, the advocacy of which was also initially linked to resistance, ultimately became a politics of participation, but it is interesting to consider where and when this ideological transformation began. I think the turning point was the struggle against the U.S.-Japan Security Treaty of 1960.

The thrust of local government changed after Japan's surrender in World War II, following the transformation of the state system by the new constitution and the Occupation reforms. The problem was no longer how to preserve liberty in the face of a central enemy; the pursuit of autonomy was now a problem of how to participate in a mass-based power structure. Both individual local governments and federations like the National Association of Governors turned into pressure groups on the state, sometimes acting singly, sometimes in combination, and sometimes even in conjunction with the All Japan Prefectural and Municipal Workers' Union.

It is interesting that both the United States and Japan are strongly imbued with the ideology of local government as independent from the state. In Japan, because the demands of local governing bodies have come to be understood as part of a pressure group process, in competition with the various other demands, there is a tendency for local government to justify itself through the freedom to oppose the state. Here, a divergence between theory (autonomy *from* the state) and reality (autonomy *vis-à-vis* the state) arises. Thus the "theories" advocated make the understanding of the reality vague.

Clearly, in America and Japan, differing political content has been invested in the concept of local government, but today the two countries are converging step by step, because the present is an era of great central policy initiative.

Deil Wright (1978) points to a dual process of federalism, in which the liberal government expands its functions and centralizes. This process has undergone three stages: a period of cooperation beginning in the 1930s, a period when policy professionalism grew within the cooperative context in the 1960s, and finally a period of federal participation through individual subsidies in the 1960s. Seen from the local (especially the municipal) level, the period of federalization that began in the 1960s has brought a proliferation of government programs. In order to carry them out, competition and regulation are essential among the agencies of the federal government and various public organizations (in the United States, this includes the Council of State Governments, National Governors' Association, National Conference of State Legislatures, National Association of County Officials, National League of Cities, U.S. Conference of Mayors, and International City Management Association; in Japan, the six federations of local officials and entities [Wright 1978: 63–65]). A Japanese-style schema in which the turf wars and sectionalism of the central bureaucracies penetrate down into the local government is completely appropriate. The central-local bargaining sphere expands, but at the same time methods are sought on the local level to regulate the confusion. If we take the federal government's system of individual subsidies as the source of this confusion, the way to regulate it would be to bring together the fractionalized individual subsidy programs and move increasingly toward broadly formed block grants in each issue

1. Coordinate Authority | 2. Inclusive Authority | 3. Overlapping Authority

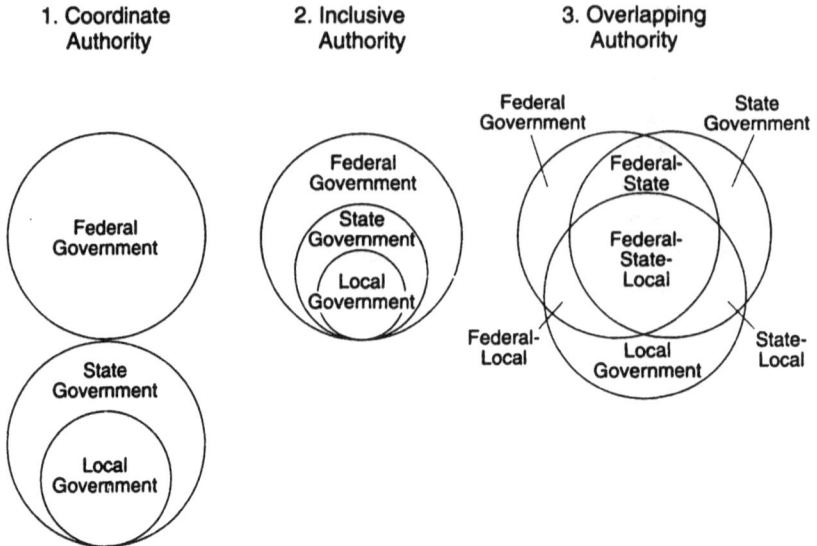

Figure 1. Deil Wright's Intergovernmental Models. *Source: Adapted from Wright 1978: 20.*

area. Indeed, for a time, U.S. subsidies from the federal government to the states and local governments changed their emphasis from categorical grants to a system of general revenue sharing (although the general revenue sharing system was halted in the mid-1970s.

Wright establishes three models to understand the connection between the three levels of government in the United States during each period; they are models of coordinate authority, inclusive authority, and overlapping authority (figure 1). The overlapping authority model is very close to the one that I advocate in this book, and I shall take up Wright's models again in chapter 5.

When looked at in this way, there are clearly great similarities between Japan and the United States. A consideration of the United States suggests the following. Even in a country where authority is separated, like the United States, in the 1930s and later the inclusive authority model became a reality, at least to some extent. The states participated in local government, federal government participated in state government, and the federal government directly participated in local government at least to some extent. Wright argues that within the federal system as it actually operated, the three levels shared the same functions, and the overlapping authority model—in which a relationship of mutual dependence pertained among the three levels—became the reality.

Japan is an example of the inclusive authority state (which subsumes Iwasaki's administrative decentralization model), as are France and Great Britain. I will discuss some of the characteristics of both of these countries' local governments below. Then a comparison with the United States will make it possible to obtain additional insights into Japanese local government. In particular, the sketches of France and Great Britain will help delineate two models for subsequent characterization of intergovernmental relations and local government in Japan.

GREAT BRITAIN, FRANCE, AND JAPAN

Among the unitary states, France and Great Britain stand in greatest contrast. In addition, because many developing nations are former French or British colonies, the two countries dominate a second order of governmental entities in the world (Alderfer 1964). Great Britain is a decentralized country that emphasizes local assemblies; France is a centralized country where central supervision permeates the localities. In France, ever since the reform from 1981 on, the executives of the second, departmental, stratum in the local system (appointed prefects) control the basic governing bodies of the first, municipal, stratum. In Japan, although it is thought that the local government system of the Meiji period was established under Prussian influence, some writers suggest that France also influenced some of its features (Katō 1980: 33–35). Given that prewar Japanese prefectural governors were appointed, this suggestion seems valid.

Great Britain. The focus of this book is on intergovernmental or central-local relations—how the central government participates in local government. In Great Britain, central-local relations are mutually independent (Lagroye and Wright 1979: chap. 1), a fact admired by Japanese scholars of local government. Traditionally in Great Britain, highly esteemed people were given honorary (unpaid) positions as chief executives or councilors, and this has been cited as an important reason for the success of the British local government system. The British system influenced the Prussian city government reforms of Heinrich Friedrich Karl vom und zum Stein in 1807, and these in turn influenced Japan when it introduced Western-style local government in the 1870s. In addition, the system that was introduced into Japan in the postwar period as part of U.S. Occupation reforms was permeated with concepts that originated in Great Britain. British local government thus influenced a number of countries and became the standard framework for many scholars. But scholars like Douglas Ashford (1982) have interpreted this mutual independence as central government indifference toward the localities and criticized it for leading to a lack of vitality in British local government. It may be, however, that political party organization is behind this lack of vitality, for in Great Britain the link between the center and the localities is the political parties, rather than the central officials, as in France.

In other words, political parties play a major role in Great Britain; as a result, the role of the individual politician recedes and the bonds of the central government are weakened. Many policy issues of local government become planks in national party platforms or campaign promises on the national level; moreover, because the central parties lead their local organizations, local vigor tends to be suppressed. The problem is that national politics enhances the potential for this to happen. For example, the national opposition party, which is in power in some local governments, often strongly opposes the ideal of central authority, as, for example, in Liverpool (Katō 1986; Nishio 1986). Conversely, the center sometimes intervenes overwhelmingly in the local system. The creation of the Greater London Council in 1965 and the metropolitan councils in 1972–74, as well as the subsequent abolition of the metropolitan councils in 1987, shows how local structures can be readily reorganized in accord with decisions made at the central party level. On the other hand, because of the existence of party channels, local legislators can rise in the party organization until they become politicians on the national level. In sum, in Great Britain the parties' mediating and restraining power is the most important link between the central and local governments.

France. In this country national paternalistic supervision (or *tutelle*) was until 1981 exercised over the municipalities by departmental prefects, who embodied the directives of the central government. The prefects oversaw the local administrative machinery, as the local agents of the state, or perhaps of government in its entirety. They were in particular agents of the Ministry of the Interior. Some reforms of this arrangement have been carried out under the Socialist government. When the reforms have been in place for some time, it will be extremely interesting to see whether they lead to major changes in French society. Yet many people think that the changes have not been that great (Becquart-Leclerc 1987).

In the case of France, the holding of concurrent positions (*cumul des mandats*) also plays an interesting role in the preservation of central-local relations. Even when he was president, Valéry Giscard d'Estaing was also a local legislator for the city of Chamalières. All the members of the lower house of Parliament are also legislators in their regions. Multiple office holders constitute only a small percentage—5–6 percent of public officials, according to Becquart-Leclerc—but the ability to serve concurrently in two public offices has given rise to a powerful group of politicians. It has been charged that this practice is the cause of the stagnation in France's democratic politics and that it creates confusion: one can conceive of a situation in which a mayor under the supervision of a prefect could himself be the minister of the interior! In such situations the prefect cannot supervise the municipalities as he is expected to. In turn, the localities have the power to influence the center through the route of concurrent office-holding. In contrast, in Japan concurrent office-holding has been quite consciously eliminated. Even running for office while holding another position is forbidden. Japan has its own system of personal networks, but they result from the practice of central officials being dispatched to work in prefectural government.

In France, bureaucrats may step down from the government to become important members of government-run enterprises or local organs. Along with the network of politicians holding concurrent positions, this personalized network of bureaucrats plays a major role (Suleiman 1978). It seems that in France standardization goes too far and must be mitigated by a social, personal network. By contrast, Great Britain fulfills its needs by institutionalizing and proceduralizing. Because its system is extremely purposeful and particularistic, with many ad hoc elements, it does not become overly standardized. That is, its flexible form allows for both universality and particularity to be harmonized.

Japan. In the case of Japan, attention focuses on the role of the Ministry of Home Affairs, which coordinates and regulates local administration, and the line ministries' top-down supervision of the local implementation of their work. ("Line" ministries have jurisdiction over policy programs, in contrast to "staff" ministries and agencies, such as the Ministry of Home Affairs and National Personnel Agency, which are not responsible for implementing programs.) In Japan the concern of the central government for local affairs is great, yet the influence of localities on the central government is also fairly strong. Here, "central" means both the line ministries and the Ministry of Home Affairs; it has also come to mean the political party in power. Thus, central-local relations are a three-way or four-way affair.

At this point, it may be worthwhile to pose several questions. First, in what way do strong central bureaucracies exercise their power? And what is their relationship to the political parties? These kinds of issues are inevitably closely related to the shape of central-local relations.

Local Leaders in the Three Countries. At the local level of government, another important point of comparison is the presence or absence of strong mayors. French mayors are the caretakers, fathers, priests, and police officers of their municipalities. Their political influence is a synthesis of the degree of financial control, their relations with the prefect, their own social status, the duration of their tenure, and whether or not they hold office in the central government (especially as a member of Parliament). In particular, their consequent positions in the political and government elite in Paris give them a mediating power between the center and locality as well as an influence not seen among British city mayors. In Great Britain, where the executive branch is part of the city council, a person whose personality symbolizes an entire locality does not usually exist. A mayor exists only as a ceremonial symbol. As a unit of self-government with the vitality to serve as the political symbol of a region, the French mayor is in a better position. In Japan, the influence of local executives, whose political authority is based on elections and vast powers delegated from the central government, is clearly greater than in the other two countries. For this reason, they frequently are targeted as the objects of influence by the center, which tries to use them for central purposes (Muramatsu 1985).

According to the preceding analysis, the links between the center and local areas are the political parties in Great Britain and the prefects, embodying central oversight, in France. Great Britain also has an administrative element in its specialist groups, and France has political elements whose influence derives from concurrent office-holding. But at the core, in Great Britain the *political* route, based on political party organization, plays the central role in intergovernmental relations; in France it is the *administrative* route, focused on the prefects. Japan certainly resembles

France in some ways, but in Japan the administrative route is not so strong. It resembles Great Britain in the salient position of political parties, but individual local politicians in Japan exert greater pressure at the national level. There is a great incentive for local politicians to act as representatives of their regions' interests vis-à-vis the state. In sum, the political and the administrative routes seem to be more or less equally blended in Japan. Japan seems to belong to Iwasaki's second (administrative decentralization) type, but even within this category, its local government seems to be on the strong side. To test this hypothesis and search for the possibility of expanding the discussion is the purpose of this book.

Local Governments: Number and Scale. In Great Britain, a series of reforms in 1972–74 reduced the number of local governments from 1,500 to 400; in France there are still more than 30,000. Accordingly, those in Great Britain are larger than those in France. As table 2 shows, Japan has followed the strategy of reducing the number while expanding their size. What are the advantages and disadvantages of this policy? In Japan, since before World War II, the government has repeatedly tried to reduce the number of towns and villages, in order to expand the financial reach of local government and make it easier to deal with any problems that arose. After the war, the number of local governments declined rapidly in 1953–54. This reduction was accomplished with the encouragement of the central government under a law for the amalgamation of towns and villages. The consolidation has been criticized as enhancing the centralization of power, but it is also possible that the expansion of the administrative and financial power of the towns and villages strengthened municipal autonomy. This is because when they reached a certain size, they could accumulate human and financial resources and their political bargaining power also increased. Moreover, this consolidation was not uniform, as was, for example, the consolidation carried out by law in Sweden in the 1970s. In Japan, it seems greater consideration was given to local conditions in consolidating municipalities. Although this consolidation is not highly regarded by Japanese scholars, it did expand the scale of local governments, and as a result, these governments have been able to cope with later urbanization.

Central-Local Relations in Three Countries: A Rough Sketch. What kind of information can we draw from this simple sketch of Great Britain and France in order to analyze Japan's local government and intergovernmental relations?

Table 2 *Changes in Number of Municipalities, 1883–1966*

Date	City	Town	Village	Total
1883	19	12,194	59,284	71,497
1889	39	15,820		15,859[a]
1898	48	1,173	13,068	14,289
1908	61	1,167	11,220	12,448
1922	91	1,242	10,982	12,315
1930	109	1,528	10,292	11,929
1940	178	1,706	9,614	11,498
Oct. 1945	205	1,797	8,518	10,520
Jan. 1950	235	1,862	8,346	10,443
Apr. 1953	280	1,953	7,808	10,041
Oct. 1955	490	1,854	2,468	4,812
Apr. 1956	495	1,870	2,303	4,668
Oct. 1960	555	1,925	1,030	3,510
Oct. 1965	560	2,000	815	3,375[b]
Apr. 1970	564	2,027	689	3,280
Apr. 1975	643	1,974	640	3,257
Apr. 1985	651	2,001	601	3,253
Oct. 1986	653	2,006	594	3,253

SOURCE: *Chihō jichi binran* (newsletter of the Home Minister's Secretariat): 18, 19, 20.
[a]Municipality system in effect.
[b]Special law for the consolidation of cities, towns, and villages in effect Mar. 29, 1965.

I think that the factors determining the character of intergovernmental relations in Japan do not reside only in the administrative relationship. The political process operates too. The administrative relationship is striking in the case of France. The central ministry bureaucracies, which make appointed prefects their agents to the municipalities, have freely—at least until 1981—exercised their supervision over mayors. Regional political claims converge in the person of the departmental assembly, creating a scenario for confrontation with the centrally appointed prefect. Of course, concurrent office-holding provides a mechanism for directly transmitting the municipalities' interests and opinions to the center, but it is only supplemental. At the departmental level, horizontally competing local political claims are set in opposition to the state's vertical control. Compromises are reached between the center and the region, with the power of each in the background. The form of this compromise is a beehive-like symbiosis, a politics that incorporates various claims and separates administration functionally at the municipal and departmental levels. Because politics and administration are in a close, symbiotic relationship, local claims are transmitted to the center and politicized there in the form of laws and ordinances. Thus, in Jean-Claude Thoenig's (1978) view, local areas "use" the center. I am unable to test the accuracy of the details of his interpretation, but it appears that he portrays a model of central-local relations in a political world where vertical administrative control is interwoven with horizontal political rivalries under administrative leadership.

In contrast, the British central government, which treats administration at the center as secondary, uses the political parties to mediate with local governments, which also treat administration at the municipal level as secondary. In the traditional view, the center was superior to local government. In fact, as the political parties gradually came to dominate the elections of local governing bodies, their role became overwhelming. The extent of central superiority is such that the "nationalization" of local politics is spoken of (Gyford and James 1983: 3). But the reality of central administration and policy does not simply subordinate local politics or force it completely into the framework of the parties. S. J. Eldersveld coined the term *stratarchy* to refer to a multilayer structure. According to Eldersveld (1964: 9), the central parties—rather than being involved in the individual regional conflicts and endangering the central organization—disperse party responsibility at the local level. Citing Eldersveld and building on his interpretation, Richard Rose (1984) divided party activity into three categories: in Parliament, at party headquarters, and within local constituencies. Party organization is an activity system in which these three elements mutually regulate each other. But Gyford and James argue that Rose has not sufficiently considered the role and position of local government activity, that he has merely crammed them into the category of "local party organization." In effect, Rose has inappropriately analyzed the role of local legislators, who oversee one-third of all governmental expenditures. In Great Britain, local legislators are also administrators, Gyford and James insist, and we must also understand this administrative aspect of their role.

Gyford and James represent central-local relations by the diagram shown in figure 2. The conventional vertical model (in Britain, a vertical party-control model) is shown by solid lines A, B, and C. It is only when we begin to take into account broken lines 1, 2, and 3, they argue, that we can understand British central-local relations. Gyford and James marshal considerable evidence for their viewpoint, but for the purpose of this

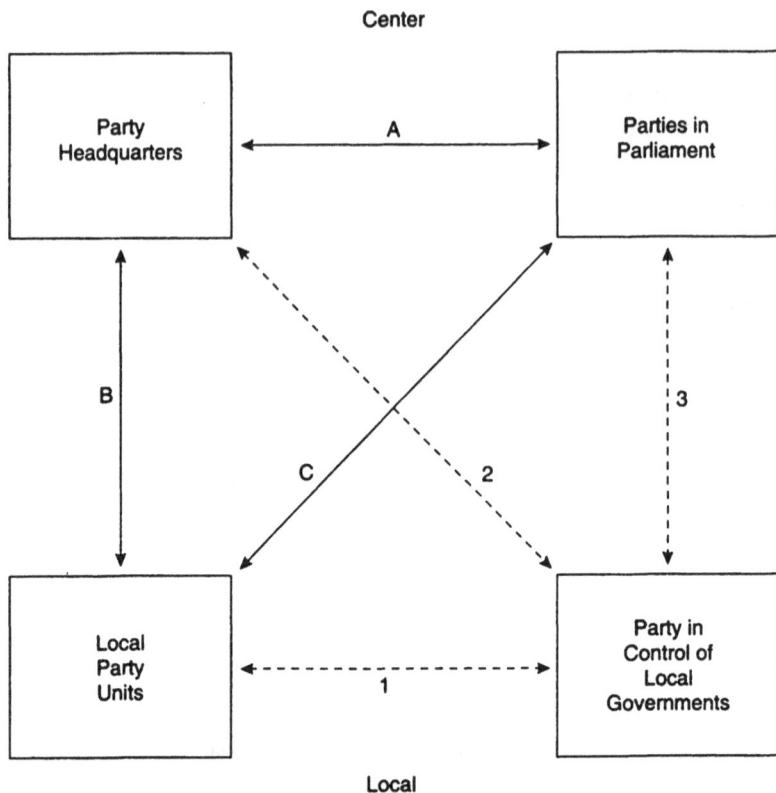

Figure 2. British Central-Local Relations. *Source: Adapted from Gyford and James 1983: 7.*

book it is sufficient to note that they are groping for an appropriate ana-
lytical model of the implication of administration and political parties
under party leaders.

As the empirical study of twentieth-century political realities in
France and Great Britain has progressed, past orthodoxies are gradually
being seen as exaggerations. In France efforts are being made to absorb
political elements into the administrative paradigm; Britain, where the
pure political-party paradigm is no longer satisfactory, is beginning to
show a concern for the role of administrative elements.

In Japan, as in France, the administration-centered theory of intergovernmental relations has been dominant until relatively recently. I call
this point of view the "vertical administrative control" model, and I be-

lieve that this model must be supplemented by elements of a political process in which local, horizontal political competition has emerged. My position is similar to that of contemporary French scholars. But it is easier to evaluate the political element in Japan, where prefectural governors have been elected for more than forty years and where the change is greater than in France, which has preserved its old system of appointive prefects, although with nominally reduced powers. In Japan, the links between the political and administrative factors are especially strong; it is in their connections that our interest lies.

Prewar and Postwar: Continuities and Discontinuities

In thinking about Japan's central-local relations and local government, we should begin our discussion with the postwar period, when local autonomy was constitutionally guaranteed for the first time. Postwar local government and central-local relations have been written about from the perspectives of political science and public administration, as well as law, finance, and other fields. But political science and public administration have transcended the partial views of law and finance and considered these issues as part of the fundamental character of the modern state.

TSUJI KIYOAKI AND NAGAHAMA MASATOSHI

Tsuji Kiyoaki has written the following about the tensions in local government during the period beginning in 1947: "With the appearance of the local government law, our local bodies were liberated from the previous restrictions of a centralized bureaucratic system into the decentralized, autonomous world, but then they confronted the new problem of reconciling local decentralization and national centralization" (1969: 119). At the same time, Rōyama Masamichi and Tanaka Jirō were making the same point (Tsuji 1969: 134), but Tsuji's essay is important for his clear view of how this reconciliation might be achieved. His view derives from John Stuart Mill's conception of central-local relations: "Power may be localized, but knowledge must be centralized" (1919: 118). Drawing on Mill, Tsuji insists that control from the center is not based on power; it should be a functional control based on information. He cites two prerequisite conditions for functional control in England: (1) the gradual establishment of the parliamentary-cabinet system created central control but did not degenerate into administrative or bureaucratic control; (2) the common social background of members of Parliament and the justices of the peace who ruled over local areas guaranteed that central and local preferences would be the same (Tsuji 1969: 123–30). According to Tsuji, when the center had to exert local control in Great Britain, it operated through legislative — or functional — control. To Tsuji, British local government seems to be the way modern local government should be. Of course, present-day British central-local relations have undergone transformation and must be perceived as part of a new relationship. But Tsuji takes Great Britain — although not necessarily Britain as it actually is — as a model, because he feels it is important to clarify the concept of "modern local government": "The first question to be settled is, what kind of reciprocal relationships portray the most typical form of modern local government?" (1969: 121). Then, in his view, we can evaluate both Japan's prewar local government and the system created in 1947 in light of the standard we have arrived at for "modern" (1969: 132–33). For a long time, social scientists proceeded from this position.

In the 1950s another work appeared on the theory of local government. Instead of evaluating present conditions by some standard of "modernity" that may not have existed, Nagahama Masatoshi's *Chihō jichi* (Local Autonomy) argues that it is more important to assign theoretical status to present-day local government (1952). Nagahama's work is one of a small number of studies that casts local government theory in present-day terms while considering various contemporary problems. He draws his examples from Great Britain and the United States and tries to find the place of Japan relative to Europe and America in the twentieth century. Even in decentralized America, the administrative control of the federal government over the states, and of the states over local government, increased in the twentieth century. In the 1930s, the all-powerful home rule movement declined, according to Nagahama. Theoretically, the danger to local government that thus arose appeared as part of a change in the basic political structure of the modern state from the opposition of state and society in eighteenth through mid-nineteenth centuries to their fusion in the twentieth century. "With this change," says Nagahama, "the traditional meaning of local government lost its foundation. Local government, which was relatively independent of state power and, moreover, acted to limit state control in mid-nineteenth century, basically became meaningless, for only when this kind of local government stands in opposition to absolutist bureaucratic state power can it claim a reason for existing" (1952: 126). Nagahama adds, "For this reason—to oversimplify—the issue for traditional local government was its *qualitative* opposition to the bureaucratic or the democratic state. In contrast, while local government during the stage of fusion of state and society presupposed democratic government, the issue it faced was a *quantitative* choice between state centralization and local decentralization" (1952: 127; italics added). That is, the relationship between the center and local government is now one of cooperation, not of opposition.

Originally written in 1947, at a time when principles of local government had become legally guaranteed, Tsuji's essay (included in his 1969 book) seems intended to discover problems within the actual local system that should be reformed according to those principles. It is critical of the central bureaucratic system's attempts to revive tutelary administration. But even in a later work (Tsuji 1976) that looks back at the postwar development of Japanese local government and takes up the proliferation of citizens' movements, Tsuji affirms that the tutelary prototype of Japanese local government remains alive at the core of the political administration, though he observes that this prototype is being forced to change. Tsuji's local government theory of the 1940s and 1950s was supported for many years. But, after detailed analysis, it appears that his theory does not always pay enough attention to the issues behind the working of more recent local government, such as the "localization" of prefectures and local opposition to the central policies.

Nagahama also does not take up contemporary problems that are directly linked to the revival of local government. For him, the local entities of the contemporary state are in principle "not bodies that perform political functions but bodies that have become completely administrative; in them, political conflict does not exist in the sense that allows political parties to exist" (1952: 266). But in actuality, both central and local governments have rejected the cooperative relationship that Nagahama's theory predicted. Local politics often becomes an arena of fierce political conflict, mediated by political parties. Of course, at the end of his book (1952: 267) Nagahama adds a "proviso" that, if the residents lose their homogeneity, local governments will become arenas of political combat. And reality has indeed followed the course suggested by the proviso. But it is not clear whether this is the kind of political confrontation that Nagahama hypothesized. Even Nagahama, who seems to be trying to make sense of the present, does not sufficiently understand the development of Japan's local government. That is probably the limitation of his method, which begins with a concept of "fundamental political structure," such as conflict of state and society or their later fusion, and deduces a variety of questions from its changing nature. As I shall discuss later, Nagahama did not foresee the frequent mediation of central-local relationships by the political parties.

More than forty years have passed since Tsuji and Nagahama tried to determine the political position of local government under the new constitutional system. The issue of forty years ago was the creation of a *legal* theory of the new local government, modeled on the Anglo-Saxon local system brought into Japan by the United States. The issue now is the formulation of a *political* theory of local government that can also make sense of the various political situations—industrialization and urbanization—that have developed since then (Matsushita 1971). The proliferation of policies and the growing complexity of policy content in industrial urban society call for changes in existing theories of local government. This book is a first step in the search for a new theory of local government.

First, however, I would like to offer a few additional comments on the two theories of central-local relations current during the early postwar period. Tsuji Kiyoaki's (1969) view, later adopted by a number of scholars who derived a hope for liberalism in Japan from an analysis of local government, became the conventional wisdom. As we have seen, the connection of the British model—actually an idealized model of nineteenth-century England—with Tsuji's theory of the three-stage development of modern history is clear. Civil society, like that of England, and parliamentarianism are the ideal in what can be called a liberal theory of local government. But could this be realized in contemporary Japan? Tsuji did not think that parliamentarianism, a two-party system, or a spontaneous civil autonomy would appear in the near future in Japan, with its continuities from the authoritarian centralized system of the prewar period. Because of its emphasis on prewar elements carried forward into the postwar period, his viewpoint seems a theory of prewar-postwar continuity.

In contrast, Nagahama (1952) attempts to survey the pattern of all contemporary central-local relations. But he does not consider the situation as all of a piece. He recognizes the significance of the election of governors in 1946, before the enactment of the constitution, but he also uneasily watches how the prewar bureaucratic system is carried forward into the postwar period. Already in *Chiji kōsen no shomondai* ("Problems in Gubernatorial Election," 1946), he argues that we must pay close attention to whether the restraints of the bureaucratic system survive in the new system. Even though he participated in the deliberations of the Second Reform Commission on Local Government in the late 1940s, he never supported its proposal that the position of prefectural governor should become again appointive. In his theories, Nagahama tries to envision a new era bringing an increase in the vigor of society. Given Nagahama's emphasis on a new era, his can be called a theory of "prewar-postwar discontinuity."

What are these two theories like in concrete terms? For example, how would they evaluate the growing intimacy of central-local relations in the 1960s? First, following Nagahama's interpretation, this trend toward intimacy has been described as a "new centralization" (e.g., Narumi 1982: 125). In effect, this is centralization but without the old authoritarianism; it responds to the new demands of the modern state. The concept of a new centralization was used in the United States in the 1930s (White 1938). People who approved of the era tried to see in the growing intimacy of central-local relations the idea of a welfare state or a service state, which had, since the New Deal, enjoyed international approval.

In the divergent interpretation of Tsuji school, on the other hand, the new centralization has been seen as an undesirable enlargement of prewar elements because of its increase in agent-delegated functions and subsidies. Building on Tsuji's position, such scholars as Akagi Suruki (1978) and Satō Atsushi (1964) moved vigorously to a critique of agency-delegated functions. This critique became standard, permeating the proposals of the National Association of Governors, the National Association of City Mayors, and other such associations, with noteworthy practical implications. However, if we closely examine this second argument, it seems one-sided, because it does not sufficiently consider the political-administrative process as a whole, including the Diet, the political parties, legislators, and local assemblies. The new centralization is a phenomenon that not only the state but also the politicians enjoy. They participate in the distributive process of subsidies and other benefits from the center. The Tsuji school overemphasizes carryovers from the prewar period, and too little attention is paid to the new, changed aspects of the postwar period. In spite of the practical strengths of the second interpretation, I think that the changes observed by the first interpretation have gradually become the determinants of the postwar practice of intergovernmental relations.

Next, I would like to consider in a little more detail the perspectives that divide these appraisals of prewar-postwar continuities and discontinuities—what kind of systemic basis do they have? The answer seems to depend on the way the theories understand the first decade of the postwar period.

In this period the two models of Japan's central-local relations both had potential. As was seen with Nagahama, one possibility was to take as a model the ideas in the new constitution and the Occupation reforms. This model predicted the growth of central-local relations in the postwar period that were completely different from the prewar period. As was seen with Tsuji, the second possibility was to focus on the early 1950s and emphasize the intention of the state to reverse the reforms of the late 1940s and restore prewar conditions. It made the elements of the prewar centralized system important components of its model and predicted a reversion to the status quo ante bellum.

POSTWAR REFORMS

The postwar reforms began with the acceptance of a new system of local government. Legal interpretations diverge as to the meaning of the acceptance of the Potsdam Declaration. In postwar state formation the central issues were the meaning of the "surrender" of the state and the meaning of its reconstruction. Under these issues we must consider such fundamental questions as the meaning of "unconditional" surrender, the degree of Japanese autonomy in the reform process, and the meaning of indirect Allied rule under the Occupation. Within the overall postwar reforms, however, the local reforms are very important because they attempted to break the powerful grip of the Home Ministry in the prewar period. I will discuss this point later; for now I would like to present a summary of the postwar local reforms.

First, before the reforms by the Allied General Headquarters (GHQ) began, the Home Ministry made a number of efforts at self-reform. The experiment to elect prefectural governors was one of these. But the Occupation army's concept of reform was far more thoroughgoing, and despite the resistance of the Home Ministry bureaucrats, its reform plan was incorporated as legal principle and finally became part of the Japanese political structure through the new constitution and laws. The old system was gradually removed, as seen in the dismantling of the Home Ministry and the neighborhood associations, loyal to the old system. Measures such as the election of governors, the thorough democratization of public offices by election, and the emergence of local assemblies as the final decision-making bodies for important local policies decisively determined the character of the postwar local system. Another major change was the partial introduction of direct democracy in the form of referendum and recall. The introduction of regulatory commissions—especially public safety commissions and school boards—was also based on the new value system. In addition, adoption of a system for ensuring fair election procedures and a governmental auditing system had considerable significance. In this way, Japan's local government was completely changed. Moreover, the basic principles of these systems were guaranteed by articles in Chapter 8 of the constitution.

Second, a counter to the main thrust of the postwar reforms was the opposition of the Home Ministry, which caused the revision of numerous points in the initial GHQ proposal. Also, when Japan regained its independence under the 1951 San Francisco Peace Treaty, the government attempted to alter its course in a number of ways. This revision was not limited to the sphere of local government but extended to such broad policy areas as antitrust and labor law; during this period, many steps amounting to a "reverse course" were taken. Compared with the reforms of the 1945–50 period, which marked the highest point of democratization, this new course, which began when Japan regained its independence, was retrograde.

The studies of Amakawa Akira (1979) and Akagi Suruki (1978) allow us to consider the problems that the Japanese side raised during the enactment of the constitution and the local government laws. One problem was how to accomplish the election of governors and, within this context, the ability of the state to carry out its own aims in relation to local government. First, the election of governors. In March 1946, after a revision of the old regulations, the first gubernatorial elections were held, before they were actually required by the constitution. At that time the concern of the officials who formed the nucleus of government was less over the procedure than over who won the elections. Out of the forty-six newly elected governors, twenty-four were previously appointed governors who had retired just before the elections. Second, the status of the governors is a problem that goes to the core of Japan's central-local relations. When the regulations were revised in 1947 the governors, though now elected, were given the rank of *kanri,* or "state official." This designation ensured their obedience to the orders or instructions of the state. In that capacity, governors were required to abide by the instructions from the center. But when the first postwar Diet deliberated on this regulation, it attached a supplementary decision: the status of state officials would apply to governors only until March 1948. Thus the problem now became whether or not the central government could fulfill its intentions toward the prefectures and municipalities once the governors became *kōri*, or *"public* officials." After foundering on the reef of this issue, the First Advisory Council on the Local Government System, created in 1946, was temporarily unable to continue its deliberations.

The Home Ministry bureaucrats lamented the "inefficiency" brought about by local decentralization, but they also were well aware that "democratization" was an inevitable trend. The harmonization of "efficiency and democratization" of the late 1940s—a political science issue posed by scholars of public administration—was already an established topic by this time. After lengthy deliberation, the resolution of the question took the form of agency-delegated functions. Agency delegation, used before the war in relation to elected mayors, was expanded to include governors as a way of imposing the state's will on elected officials. After reaching this resolution, the Japanese officials who were negotiating with GHQ relaxed, and the First Advisory Council on the Local Government System could easily draw up its report. As a result, stipulations reinstating the prewar duties of prefectural governor were placed in Article 2 of the local government law, along with special and delegated duties. A proviso was added to Article 2 to the effect that agency delegation to the heads of legally based public entities was to be freely exercised. This proviso gave central ministries a tool to exercise supervision over localities.

In the 1960s this proviso about agency-delegated functions became linked to a rising number of delegated functions concerning city planning, the management of environmental pollution, the disposal of industrial wastes, and the like. At the same time state subsidies to local government were increasing; together these two trends were bringing about a "new centralism." The pressures of agency-delegated functions enhanced the level of centralization. Thus, even in the period after the 1960s, the prewar-postwar continuity theory argues that the "new centralization" was actually in many ways simply an extension of prewar institutions. But the increase in agency-delegated functions and subsidies in the 1960s requires a different interpretation, as I discuss below.

Let us return once more to the beginning of the story. According to Akagi, continuity between the prewar and postwar periods was built into the new system from the time that agency-delegated functions were adopted in the new local government law in the process of creating the postwar Japanese constitution. The process was strengthened by the "reverse course" that began when the peace treaty of 1951 was signed.

In 1953 a law was enacted for the amalgamation of towns and villages, reducing the number of local governments in Japan by two-thirds. Japanese political scientists criticized the consolidation for obstructing the growth of local democracy because it made access to decision making in local government remote and inconvenient. In 1954, with the new police law, the abolition of municipal police departments was completed, and jurisdiction over public safety was moved to the prefectural level, to the prefectural safety commissions. Prefectural police chiefs became national, not local, officials. In 1955 a local finance reconstruction law was enacted, providing for strict central regulation of the administrative operations of local entities designated as "local governments to be financially reconstructed." In 1956 the school board law was revised and the election of members was changed to a system of appointments. Earlier, in 1952, the selection of ward mayors in metropolitan Tokyo, which had been by election, changed to a form of indirect selection based on the recommendation of the Tokyo metropolitan assembly with the consent of the governor. This change made it possible for the metropolitan government to limit the autonomous authority of the wards; moreover, because the metropolitan governor at the time was one link in a conservative political network with strong ties to the central government, it clearly strengthened central control.

Some people might also cite that year's settlement of the "special cities" problem as an example of how the will of the center was strengthened. The special municipalities problem goes back to the prewar municipal system—or, more precisely, to 1888, when Japan first introduced an election system for municipal public offices. But it arose more directly in part of the report of the First Advisory Council on the Local Government System, which included a section stating that the governmental prerogatives of prefectures should be given to a group of "special municipalities," understood to be Osaka, Kyoto, Nagoya, Yokohama, and Kobe. Part 3, Section 1, of the Local Government Act set up the "special cities" category and gave them the same status and scope of power as prefectural governments. GHQ was sympathetic to this idea. Leaving a detailed analysis of the situation, background, and politics of this system to other scholars (Katō 1981; Okazaki 1981), I will simply relate here that the movement of 1948–49 came to naught because the prefectures were strongly opposed to making the five cities into special municipalities. What put an end to the debate at this time was an interpretation of Article 95 of the constitution, which stipulated that any law pertaining to a *particular* locality had to be submitted to a popular vote of the people of that area. Once the interpretation was made that "particular locality" referred to prefectures, not the five municipalities concerned, the setback for the municipalities was obvious, given the population distribution within prefectures concerned, and they had to abandon the plan. The movement was reactivated in 1952, but the retrograde ("reverse course") trends of this period meant that emphasis on the prefectures strongly predominated. Finally, the five municipalities had to agree that the transfer of sixteen prefectural functions to them was sufficient. Thus a movement to enlarge the powers of local government ended in a victory for the center, which created a framework for central-local relations that deemphasized the five municipalities.

After resolution of the special cities issue in 1956, the return to an appointive gubernatorial system became intertwined in 1957 with the issue of creating a system of regions—government units including several prefectures—as a way of reforming the system. But after the discussions of prefectural reform in this period, "debates over uniform national wide-scale regional administration gradually disappeared" (Nishio 1979: 224). The cities gave up on the special municipality system, and the center gave up on the appointment of governors. I think that postwar central-local relations reached a balance at this time. Afterward, there was a tendency for the issue of power distribution to be limited to specific concerns and sporadic movements. Japan entered an era when systems were used, not formed.

To summarize: For people who see prewar-postwar continuities, the special characteristics of Japan's local government are agency-delegated functions and the newly created laws supporting a reverse course. By contrast, those who see prewar-postwar discontinuity emphasize that postwar political society adopted democratization as its basic framework. This adoption was enforced in state-level structural changes such as the transformation from imperial sovereignty to popular sovereignty and the establishment of the Diet as "the sole law-making organ of the state" (Article 41 of the Japanese constitution); at the local level, it meant that elections became the sole, supreme method of selecting leaders and legislators. Local government has undergone significant "politicization" in a modern sense, as interpreted by the discontinuity school, and as a result the political aspects of central-local relations have gradually become important.

CHAPTER 2

Central-Local Relations

Old and New Theories

The Vertical Administrative Control Model

The previous chapter traced the development of Japan's local government since the prewar period from a comparative perspective. What kind of political actor has it been in the postwar period? What kind of theory is appropriate to understand it? First, I will analyze the dominant theory or the centralization paradigm, which emphasizes the centralizing aspects of the central-local relationship; then I will raise my doubts about it and advance a new theory in which local political penetration into the central government is regarded as important.

First, the dominant theory makes the following assertions. In spite of the constitutional provisions guaranteeing local autonomy, the role of local government in the postwar period has been reduced in terms of political reality. In Japan there is no local government comparable to that of such Anglo-Saxon countries as the United States, which exemplifies the "separationist model" of local government. To explain the lack of local autonomy, many scholars point to legal structure, which allows for an increase in agency-delegated functions and, perhaps even more important, the exercise of financial control through central government subsidies. The fact that more than half of local government revenue comes from Tokyo has been used to demonstrate the weak financial power of Japanese local government. Thus, in the centralization paradigm that I refer to as the vertical administrative control model, local government is always in a subordinate position.

In my opinion, the vertical administrative control model is most valid for considering the central-local relations that took shape from 1945 to 1955, when Japan was still under reconstruction and much of the prewar system continued to function. However, in this period, especially after the early 1950s, local political dynamism started to change the nature of the system toward another model, here called the interdependent relationship model, which accounts for the local influence over the decisions in Tokyo as well. First, I will examine the elements of the administrative control model, which will be eventually counted as part of the interdependent relationship model.

ELEMENTS OF THE VERTICAL ADMINISTRATIVE CONTROL MODEL

Japan's central-local relations during the early postwar period have been considered as an age of bureaucracy, when the administrative link between the center and local government was the main or only link between the two levels. Scholars in this period questioned whether the administrative connection was part of a universal phenomenon in industrialized countries and Japan was following that route. In the United States, politically, the connection through the parties and the legislative branch was the main element that integrated the federal, state, and local governments (Nagahama 1952: 68–72). But even in the United States the connection, based on financial grants and other administrative controls, between federal-state and state-local levels was only gradually introduced—after the Depression, the New Deal, and World War II—changing the nature of U.S. intergovernmental relations. Observing this change, Nagahama considered central-local relations in the contemporary state to be a "cooperative" relationship based on administrative control (1952: 140). But unlike the pattern of central-local relations in the other industrial democracies, that in Japan includes shared functions in which authority is not completely given to local governments (Muramatsu 1975b; see also the fusion theory described in Amakawa 1983). In many policy areas, through agency delegation and categorical grants, all three levels—national, prefectural, and local government—are responsible for the same functions.

The first element to consider in the vertical model is the agents of delegated powers. These have been the governors and mayors alone; initially, even though local assemblies could debate about the conditions of the implementation of delegated tasks, the legal structure made it impossible for them to participate in decision making regarding these tasks (the law was later revised, making it easier for them at least to give opinions). This mode of implementation has stood at the center of Japan's central-local system and contributed to maintaining the unity of political society on the national level. To be effective, this system requires at least that there be mayors and governors who favor "direct ties" to the central government. If the mayors and governors are backed by local assemblies, the system is more efficient. Yet even if the supporters of the mayors and governors become the minority in the assemblies and councils, as long as the mayors and governors profit from legal arrangements tied to the central ministries, the system cannot be destroyed. But if this underlying condition changes, there is no doubt that the actual functioning of this system would change. Such a change will be discussed later, in relation to the 1970s, when a new phase of Japanese local government was ushered in by the leftist ascendancy of the 1960s.

The second element of the model is financial relationships. It is thought that local governing bodies' chronic financial needs and the central government's fulfillment of these needs by subsidies and by its authority to issue bonds creates a position of superiority for the center over localities. The limitations set on the taxing authority of local governments are also cited as reasons for the inferior position of local government. Within this financial framework is born a "sadomasochistic" vicious circle (Akagi 1978: 19), wherein local governments are psychologically dependent on the center and central bureaucrats are doubtful of local capacities for independence. For a long time, even though the problems of this system were pointed out, it was not changed. But the advance of urbanization to a new stage, "metropolitanization," and the changes in the political structure that required the creation of the 1981 Second Provisional Administrative Reform Commission (Rinji Gyosei Chosakai, or Daini Rinchō) and its successors—all made a thorough examination of the system necessary. It must be noted that this financial system is part of the overall structure of central-local relations, which is built around the theory of agency-delegated functions.

The third element in the vertical administrative control model is the administration of personnel. The system whereby administrative officials are dispatched from the center to work for the prefectures makes it easy to enforce on the local level administrative standards established at the national level. In the United States as well, there are mechanisms that make uniform administrative standards possible. For public officials, organizations of specialists in the field to which they belong are very important as reference groups, and the standards that these organizations establish have the power to compel adoption among the rank and file of public officials in the same field all over the country. In the United States such "policy communities" are found across federal, state, and local organizations of public officials. In Japan, however, one point of debate is if we can even conceptualize a "community" of policy specialists in fields crossing the levels of government, because some hierarchical relationships in the specialists' group may be a barrier to any community atmosphere. Therefore, for example, in the case of Japan, some observers say that "career bureaucrats" are more important than "policy communities" for linking the center and the local areas. While many of these officials are "permanent residents" in the central bureaucracy until they retire, they go back and forth between the center and the various prefectural offices while climbing the ladder of advancement. This practice is an important line of communication for problems and policy orientations between the center and the local areas. With regard to the future of Japan's local governments, it is of considerable importance whether the social networks arising from this system become refined into U.S.-style policy communities as discussed above or whether they continue as status relationships. In any case, the personnel of the Ministry of Home Affairs, which links the center and the localities (especially the prefectures)—as well as officials in other ministries and agencies—must be scrutinized for their ability to maintain the effective implementation of policy.

The fourth element in the vertical administrative control model, which combines the first three, is the dynamics of the administrative process. The administration of the central government overall is composed of two processes. The first is the actual implementation of policies already determined by laws and other regulations. The implementation process in a country like Japan, whose government has broad discretionary powers and a long history of the practice of administrative guidance, has a strong inherent potential for slack on the part of the agencies and tends to invite local political intervention. But more important than the setting of the policy-making process is a second factor—the preparation by each ministry of a draft of its budget for the coming year. Here the ministries' goals for the coming year are examined, and it is decided which concerns should be featured in the central public policies. Then these targets are made concrete in the budget for the coming year. Because many operations in central public policies are delegated to local governing bodies, the central bureaucrats who prepare the national government's budget must listen to the concerns and needs of the local areas through a series of negotiations and consultations—"hearings" with local officials. By this process, the people in charge of the budget of each ministry can acquire precise information about the importance of their various budget provisions. It is well known that both the schedule for determining the budget of the central government and its content influence the formation of local government budgets, but it is also true that the counter-process, the hearing process, provides local governments with a means of communicating their needs to the central government.

THE VERTICAL ADMINISTRATIVE
CONTROL MODEL EXAMINED

The structure of the vertical administrative control model I have just described continues to exist in Japan's central-local relations. But one must note that since the conservative merger of 1955, when the Jiyu Minshu To, or Jimintō (Liberal Democratic Party, or LDP), was formed, in addition to the administrative route, another route linking local politics to the national level has gradually developed. This route has been created by political dynamism, and a possible criticism of the previous interpretation is its lack of a political perspective. Specifically, the previous model pays very little attention to the activities of groups of politicians, especially locally elected members of the Diet, who connect local interests to the decision making of the central government. And a second criticism is that theories on local government have so far paid insufficient attention to political processes within local government.

As for the first critique, beginning in 1955, local governments and local politicians engaged in vigorous lobbying during the budget-drafting process at the national level. With the strong, centrally appointed governors before the war, there was pressure by local interest groups on the prefectural level, but after the war, especially after 1955, it became directed at the central government (Masumi 1969: chap. 4). Many political scientists interpret this politicization of the budget process by local politicians as a strengthening of the power of the conservative parties in relation to the central bureaucracy. Under this new process, which increased in importance in the 1960s, the people in charge of preparing the budgets for the central agencies collaborated with the various committees of the LDP Policy Affairs Research Council (Seimu Chosakai). Local appeals and pressure were aimed not only at the central agencies but also at the conservative party and especially at committee members of the Policy Affairs Research Council or other party members in the Diet. We can see this change as the appearance of a political route, in contrast to the previous administrative route. This interpretation has gained currency since I first presented it (Muramatsu 1975c), but studies of the political processes within local government are still rare. One excellent study is by Yorimoto Katsumi (1985), who pays attention not only to the usual local executives, legislatures and political parties, and bureaucratic groups, but also to civil servants' unions. He found that the role of unions marked the point of greatest difference between local and central administration.

Building on the foregoing, we can analyze the theoretical structure of the vertical administrative control model. First, let us take up the "vertical" aspect of the theory. Although this theory has never been precisely defined by its proponents, Richard Samuels (1983) summarizes it from an examination of extreme cases. According to him, an important aspect of this theory is that parts of the central bureaucratic system give orders and commands to related departments in local governing bodies. Exchanges of opinions within or between local groups have very little influence. There are no horizontal relations between either central or local administrative organs, and the compartmentalized flow of paternalistic administrative orders, along with central ministries' sectionalism, heightens existing rivalries at the local level, making it impossible for local governing bodies to enforce coordination or to preserve cooperation.

Many scholars think that vertical administration at the center resulted from the ministries' sectionalism and expanded to the local levels (e.g., Satō 1964: 195–98). Proponents of the vertical administrative control model argue that this system originated in the prewar period, or to be more precise, during the war period itself. But the vertical administration theory has elements that cannot be explained without reference to the postwar period and the abolition of appointive governors with which it began. As Samuels (1983) says, the vertical administration theory means that, as the sectionalism of the central ministries and agencies descends to the prefectures and municipalities through their respective local departments, it becomes difficult to form and execute unified, coordinated policies among the related departments within the administrative structures of the prefectures and municipalities. Under prewar central-local relations—a system in which appointed governors were single-handedly responsible for transmitting the orders of the center to the local areas and conversely monopolized the transmission of local needs and problems to

the center—the sectionalism of the center did not extend to the municipalities; it stopped at the prefectural level. Liaison between the various
departments of the central ministries and the municipality as a whole was
controlled by the governors. The governors' influence made it possible to
coordinate the conflicting interests in the central ministries. Thus, it is apparent that the vertical administrative control model includes elements
that arose out of postwar changes. The conversion from appointed to
elected governors strengthened local representation, but at the same time
it invited division and competition along ministerial lines.

A broader understanding of sectionalism is thus necessary. It cannot
merely refer to struggles for legal authority within the bureaucratic system but should be seen as a reflection of the diverse power structure created when ministry-related interest groups or groups of politicians (such
as factions) join in alliances with administrative bodies. The center is not
a monolithic entity (Muramatsu 1981b: chap. 3).

In many ways the central ministries serve as "superordinate" organs
that supervise and lead the local administrations, particularly when central programs are being implemented. At the local level, legislatures are
weaker than at the national level and administrative bureaus are strongly
influenced by the central ministries in carrying out their duties. This is
certainly propitious territory for the vertical administrative control
model. But local executives are also able to use this vertically divided situation in their dealings with their own legislature (assemblies and councils). Executives or bureaus with discretionary powers can fall back on
the expressed intentions of the central government, or on the fact that
some task is delegated by an agency, in responding to questions or demands from assemblies or councilors. For local administrative authorities it is easier to deal with central controls, which may have complicated
procedures but do not penetrate deeply into the substance of implementation, than with a legislature, which may want to interfere in the substance itself. Moreover, it seems to me that within the vertical administrative structure governors and mayors freely make their own programs
into government policy.

On the whole, proponents of the vertical administrative control model
analyze local governments in Japan with a critical eye. They ask, "Why is
there no local government in Japan like that of Europe or the United
States?" In searching for solutions to this problem, political scientists
have proposed reform plans reflecting visions of Anglo-Saxon local
government—the British separationist model in particular—that do not

necessarily correspond to reality. In their view, Japan is too central-ized, while British local government is decentralized, as a modern state should be.

Two objections can easily be raised. The first concerns whether Japan is really all that centralized. I have had countless opportunities to ob-serve local governing bodies in western Japan in a variety of decision-making situations, and they do not appear to be receiving a succession of orders from the central government regarding important decisions per-taining to their independence. In fact, we can say that Japanese local governments function rather autonomously.

At least we can say that there are too few empirical studies examining the present situations in European and U.S. local governments to draw this conclusion. Moreover, there is a lack of serious analyses of "auton-omy." What degree of local autonomy is there in Europe and the United States—and under what definition of autonomy? At the present stage of research on local autonomy, it does not seem that many conclusions really have a "comparative" basis.

In general, as I have indicated, current local government theories rest on an assumption of prewar-postwar continuity, that systems, proce-dures, habits, beliefs, and practices carried over from the prewar period lie at the core of the vertical administrative control model. The assertion of continuity is also based on the attitudes of central and local bureau-crats and city dwellers as well as the legal and financial reliance of local cities on the center. We can, however, advance a counterargument, citing phenomena that the continuity theory cannot explain. The increase in influence and political importance of mayors and governors, the politi-cal pressure-group activities that originated in postwar democracy and mobilized locally elected Diet members, and the vigorous political processes emerging at the local level (for example, citizens' movements related to pollution), none of these could be predicted from the vertical administrative control model. If we take account of "politics," we see in-formation and influence flowing from localities to the center as well as the other way around. I think we need a new model.

From Horizontal Political Competition to Overlapping Authority

The element to be emphasized in this new model is politics. Politics, however, seems to have its effects in opposing directions, sometimes strengthening and sometimes weakening the administrative control of central governments. In any case, the new model that I will develop here envisions a relationship of overlapping authority in which central-local relations are mediated in part by politics. I am not saying that the traditional vertical administrative control model is completely mistaken. Rather, I have tried to create a model that includes not only the elements of the traditional vertical administrative control model, but also the central-local political structure and the processes created by politicians. This new model of "horizontal political competition" is a first step toward my final proposal of an interdependent relationship model of the Japanese central-local relationship. To deepen an understanding of this point of view, I will examine two developments, drawing on concrete cases from the 1950s, 1960s, and 1970s. The first involves a new interpretation of the central-local relationship in the age of regional development, a period that can be considered compatible with the vertical administrative control model. The second looks at local government during the period of citizens' movements and leftist local governments.

COOPERATION AND REGIONAL DEVELOPMENT

The economic development of postwar Japan began at the local level in the form of local development policy. During this period, a study appeared that looked for the first time at the local level of government in terms of the political process—Ōhara and Yokoyama's *Sangyō shakai to seiji katei* (Industrial Society and Political Processes, 1965). This work emphasizes the central government's control over local areas in the implementation of industrial policy, but it also analyzes political processes at the local level that blend the power of business and labor. Moreover, it is extremely perceptive in its analysis of actual relationships. This perspective, however, was quickly swallowed up in a flood of orthodox studies based on the vertical administrative control model.

Because of the way regional development issues were dealt with in this period, Japan's central-local relations played a pivotal role, making communication efficient between the political world, the bureaucracy, business, and agricultural groups. Within the huge process that encompassed all regions, the role of state was still vigorous, but at the same time the influence of business was expanding. In central-local relations, the regional voice was growing stronger. These changes in power relations had been set in motion by an expansion of the influence of the political parties over the bureaucratic system, which followed in turn from the policy-making processes launched by the cabinet in 1962 in the Comprehensive National Development Plan (Zenkoku Sogo Kaihatsu Keikaku, or Zenso), a turning point that encouraged the participation of these various actors.

The Zenso was formulated by the following process. First, as part of Prime Minister Ikeda's plan to double the national income, a group of representatives from government, bureaucracy, and economic advisory councils formed a plan for the "rational" spatial placement of industry. It stated that new investment should be concentrated in the Pacific Belt area, but outside of the Tokyo and Osaka areas. As this plan was taking shape, Diet members from agricultural areas quickly organized an agricultural area support association and pointed out the political importance of the backward rural areas, arguing that the most important policy issue confronting Japan should be the correction of interregional income inequalities. The association opposed concentrating investment in the Pacific Belt area; as a result of its insistence, correcting interregional income inequalities was written into the Zenso of 1962 as its most important goal. As a result, an unexpectedly large number of development areas—thirteen in all—were designated, and a decision was made to disperse the investment (Masumi 1969: 413).

The process of designating regions in order to implement a new law promoting the construction of industrial cities, which was instituted in the same year and based on the Zenso, is a remarkable example of how pressure from the local areas caused the development plan's "rationality" to go completely astray. In the designated regions, in order to make public investment effective, large factories were to be moved from the Tokyo and Osaka metropolitan areas. As a result of the construction of new factories, whose stimulating effect was to extend to local industry, regional surplus labor would be absorbed by new economic activities. Again, according to the law, local governments in the designated regions would be given special consideration in the distribution of bond-issuing powers and subsidies. Consequently, the prefectures seeking regional designation mobilized local politicians and unleashed "the greatest petition war in history" (Satō 1963–64; Satō 1965: 97–118). The designated regions, originally planned as less than thirteen areas, grew to nineteen.

During this period, local governments had good reason to lure factories. First, many local governments suffered from financial deficits. The main causes were the unexpected costs of reconstruction after typhoons and other disasters as well as the expansion of public and welfare projects that accompanied the postwar recovery. Civic leaders thought their towns would be enriched by the increase in customer demand and property taxes that the new factories would bring. Second, Japan's local tax system, which makes property taxes and the corporate share of enterprise taxes a general revenue source, made bidding for factories attractive. As a result, it was said that 70 percent of all Japanese municipalities in 1966 had factory enticement ordinances that gave special privileges to the new factories. These privileges generally included the following: (1) new factories received exemptions from property taxes for three to five years; (2) the factories received donations of part of their sites; and (3) local governments carried out investments in public works (such as widening and repairing roads and improving harbors) that benefited the activities of the factories.

I do not mean here to address the overall reasons for Japan's economic growth, but I should point out that the lead of the central ministries, using the central-local structure described above, was effective in strengthening regional industrial reception systems. The broad policy of LDP, the party in power, was to rely for national defense on the U.S.-Japan Security Treaty and make economic development the state's goal, and it used the integrated structure skillfully in relation to local government to pursue this goal. Moreover, by this process, the party in power succeeded in ingraining itself deeply into the administrative side of central-local relations.

What were the results of regional development carried out with these intentions? Japan achieved a high rate of development and became one of the world's great economic powers. The cities became centers of socioeconomic activity by spatially integrating land, capital, and labor. But the concentration of people in the large cities created a number of urban problems, which eventually became a major point of political contention. However, that came later, along with the serious problem of depopulation—the reverse side of overpopulation (Nishio 1979). For now, let us take up the results of development that directly impinged on politics or administration.

First, there was a reformation of conservative local power structures. Power gradually moved from local notables to groups that understood the development of modern industry. Even though this change can be seen at the prefectural level, it originated at the municipal level. For example, in the case of the city of Kariya, studied by Akimoto Ritsuo (1971), the city had been dominated by two illustrious families, but with the expansion of the Toyota automobile industry, people connected with

Toyota began to gain power. When the danger of a split between the two groups that made up the conservative faction in the city council emerged, powerful people connected to the Toyota corporation acted as mediators. From this time the power structure of the city changed to one based on the new industries (Akimoto 1971: 181–87).

Second, the power of the LDP headquarters vis-à-vis its local party chapters increased. For an example, let us look at Chiba prefecture (Ōhara and Yokoyama 1965: 39–42; Ide 1972: 94–132). Before the national development plan was drawn up, this prefecture was pursuing its own regional economic development independently by such means as bids to the Kawasaki Steel Corporation. And Tokyo's large corporations also had a strong interest in this region as an industrial belt adjacent to the city. The gubernatorial election of 1958 became important because business considered political conditions key to the realization of these plans; attention focused on Governor Shibata, who was running for re-election. Until this time, he had been the official candidate of the Socialist Party, but because he continued to promote the large-scale development of the eastern part of Chiba prefecture, he was gradually persuaded by LDP prefectural headquarters to run as an LDP candidate, and as such he won in 1958. But Shibata also thought it necessary to preserve Chiba's agricultural land in spite of its economic development, and the LDP and business circles that wanted still more economic development later on began to consider him an obstacle. In the gubernatorial election of 1962 the LDP headquarters withdrew its official backing of Shibata; he ran as an independent, but was defeated.

Third, as the importance of planning and policy based on rational calculation increased, so did the importance of statistical planning for local government. And the importance of experts increased proportionately. Prefectures and municipalities became concerned about training experts in urban problems, statistics, and computers.

Fourth, even when regional governments were not particularly systematic in forming regional development plans, making bids to factories, and analyzing the consequences of these activities, their calculation of the benefits and costs of policies and decisions turned out to have major significance. It provided an opportunity to look hard and ask what kinds of results their own decisions had brought about, what kinds of concerns the central government had for the regions, and what it had done for or to them. (For example, these considerations are reflected in the revisions of the comprehensive development plans made by various local governments in the 1970s.)

The participants in decisions about economic development were the policy-based factions (or *zoku*) within the LDP, individual LDP and other conservative politicians, the central ministries, and corporations, as well as local governments and their related interest groups. There was a strong tendency to exclude the Socialist Party and other opposition parties as well as labor unions from the decision-making process. Masumi Junnosuke (1969) calls this the "usual" form of decision making, in contrast to the "unusual" form—the politics of violent opposition of left and right that emerged in such instances as the police law in 1957 or the U.S.-Japan Security Treaty of 1960. I have amplified this interpretation, describing how it expands into the concepts of "ideological" versus "policy-making" processes (Muramatsu 1981b: 290); here I would like to repeat my discussion with an eye on government at the local level. The bone of contention in the "usual" or "policy-making" form of decision making is the distribution of benefits such as subsidies of various kinds, the ways in which participants redistribute the benefits they receive within their own groups. These, to borrow a term from public economists, are "divisible" benefits. The slogan raised by conservative candidates in the 1960 local elections—"Direct ties to the center"—was an ostentatious demonstration that they were participants in the "usual" decision-making process described above. "Direct ties to the center" is one important characteristic of central-local relations within the "usual" system. But the politics of regional development mobilize not only central-local government relations, but also political relations, including those with the parties and the members of the legislatures.

In contrast to the LDP's focus on benefits, for a long time the object of opposition parties' concern was ideology. Opposition parties, unable to distribute benefits based on government public policies, rallied their forces with ideology. Their high point was the security treaty struggle of 1960. Their idealism, which was subtly linked to nationalism, seems to have gained the sympathy of a rather large number of people. But we should note that their failure in the treaty struggle also became a pivotal point that turned the opposition parties' concern toward regional issues. The candidacy of Asukata Ichio, who resigned from the lower house of the Diet to run for mayor of Yokohama in 1963, was the first important event in this movement. Some of those who had participated in the peace treaty struggle, after reflecting on why they had not been able to obstruct the treaty's revision, concluded that the average citizen in the provinces did not understand the importance of the issue. It was necessary to politicize the citizens. Finally, under this logic, they reasoned that politicization of people could be accomplished only by wrestling with local issues like roads and sanitation. Therefore the opposition parties gradually moved from ideological to concrete politics and began passionately to address local problems. This was the period when pollution problems—the by-product of high-speed industrial growth—were intensifying everywhere, and it was natural for "local democrats" (Matsushita 1961) to launch an attack on them. During this period, the opposition parties were also important because they promoted welfare policies. And local governments had the financial power to adopt redistribution policies of their own.

CONFLICT OVER THE ENVIRONMENT AND WELFARE

During the late 1960s, Japanese politics—national and local—underwent a period of change. A number of problems appeared in the cities, and the need for new policies spurred on political changes. The experience of this period makes clear the need for a new model that includes politics in the understanding of central-local relations.

Rising income, an increase in the population of central cities and suburbs, and an increase in automobile ownership were all material signs that appeared after the period of rapid economic growth. Leisure as well as work became important. But on the other hand, the negative aspects of rapid industrial expansion became obvious. There is no limit to the examples that could be given—dissatisfaction with the quantity and quality of housing, difficulties in commuting, inadequate water, the now-visible inadequacy of city planning. Until the early 1970s, although contaminated air and water were seen as pollution problems, people stressed the benefits of concentration rather than the disadvantages of congestion. Environmental pollution changed the atmosphere completely (on these issues, refer to *Kikan gendai keizai* 1974: vol. 3, no. 15). People began to argue that serious consideration must be given to individual values, not to "the state," and to their quality of life, not to manufacturing. In the words of a TV commercial, the sensibilities had changed "from hard work to beautiful life." The rise in income and increase in leisure turned the eyes of urban residents to the environment and contributed to the emergence of an active citizens' movement.

One reason for successful economic growth that has hardly been touched on is the continued stability of the political system centered on the Liberal Democratic Party (Muramatsu and Krauss 1987). The central-local relations described in the vertical administrative control model alone could not have generated the wide support needed for regional development. Mobilization of related factors through the political process was needed. The fact that the opposition parties were not active participants in the process probably guaranteed the efficiency of decision making. But as urban problems came to be regarded as serious, Masumi's "usual" decision-making process had to change. "Disadvantages" began to be discussed along with "benefits" in the policy-making process, and economic debates began to take negative externalities—not just profits—into consideration. Under these conditions, the opposition parties gained in power. In central-local relations, in contrast to the LDP's boastful election slogan of "direct ties to the center," opposition candidates began to stress "direct ties to the citizens." In some cases LDP candidates even had to drop their slogan. Local elections seemed to turn a corner with the Kyoto gubernatorial election of 1970 and the Tokyo gubernatorial election of 1971. The Kyoto candidate Shibata Mamoru and the Tokyo candidate Hatano Akira, who both emphasized "direct ties to the center," lost in spite of all-out campaigns supported by the LDP. Even in the nonurban conservative bastions, support for the central government ceased to be firm. The promises publicized in many regional development projects had not brought benefits to the local areas as expected. Even in some areas where big industry actually invested, the benefits did not materialize because the very incentives of property tax reductions and exemptions offset the amount of income expected. Some municipalities were already in a difficult situation due to preinvestment; and despite expectations of expanded local employment, the new factories were not interested in unskilled local labor (Nishio 1979). Local governments felt they had to carefully examine the central government's plans and leadership, including their costs. They learned that they had to exercise great caution in making decisions.

Among the political issues in local government during this period, the most important was the eruption of local citizens' movements and the wide-scale appearance of progressive local governments. Along with this came opportunities for local opposition to the heretofore dominant relationship of cooperation, based on ties to the center. Cracks began to appear in Japan's unified administrative structure of central-local relations. Let us analyze each of these shifts in detail.

Citizens' Movements. These movements were composed of groups of local residents whose actions were intended to influence government decision making; in Japan they were especially noticeable from the late 1960s to the early 1970s in the area of environmental pollution. At that time the number of these organizations ranged from several hundred to more than a thousand (see the survey in the appendix of *Shimin* 1971: vol. 1). As the effectiveness of these movements became known, innumerable new movements were formed, taking up other latent problems, and in many areas the projects of local governing bodies that depended on popular cooperation or acceptance ground to a stop.

Citizens' movements were important political events for Japan. They forced a reconsideration of the omnipotence of the policy of "GNP first," and they were a major factor in reforming a number of the long-term plans of national and local governments. The movements deserve attention because it was hoped that they would have the power to solve urban problems, beginning with environmental pollution, and also because they seem to present an antithesis to conventional understanding of Japan's "political culture" (Matsushita 1971; Shinohara 1971). It was startling when people who were expected to be obedient to government leadership and rarely to participate in politics other than in elections changed their roles and became active. For just that reason careful case studies are needed of the participants in citizens' movements, their organizational modes, and the characteristics of the leadership. Fortunately, superb studies have been published by such American political scholars as Margaret McKean (1981).

Generally speaking, Japanese movements from the late 1960s on can be divided into movements in urban areas and those in nonurban areas. The former can be called preventive movements. Usually, their participants were people who benefited from a rise in their standard of living as the result of economic growth policies. The rise in income standards led to demands for a better environment. Because the seriousness of the urban problems that accompanied rapid urbanization was without precedent in other countries, the methods of drawing attention to these problems were often radical. But although the actions were radical, the citizens' movements had a conservative intent. Their "enemy" was not only industry but any and all public or private systems damaging the quality of the environment. This type of citizens' movement was thus concerned not simply with environmental pollution but also with city planning, protecting natural and cultural assets, and a broad range of urban issues. The right-to-sunlight movement is an example of the fight against the high-rise policy of city governments. In another example, a giant petrochemical complex was rejected by citizens in the city of Mishima, in Shizuoka prefecture. Similarly, the new residents of a Kyoto suburb forced the Ministry of Construction to abandon its plans for a highway extension in the area. What should be noted is not the ferocity of these movements but the fact that their core was middle class. What does this radicalization of the middle class (Apter 1971: 36–80) mean? Perhaps it is the increase in the number of people with tangible assets who needed a movement to protect these assets that warrants attention. Yet, for some people, intangible rewards were a larger factor: increased leisure time and access to information made political activism possible for the first time. The general unease of the middle class in the era of rapid growth could be felt. A precise analysis of this is not our topic here, but the new political attitude of urban residents brought to Japanese politics a new flexibility—and a correlated instability.

In contrast, the local citizens' movements that arose in farming and fishing villages showed some of the characteristics of human rights movements. The citizens of farming and fishing villages are generally obedient to government leadership. Farming and fishing regions as a whole accepted the economic growth policy of government. Thus in 1972 Prime Minister Tanaka could confidently present his idea for a total spatial relocation of industries in Japan. This development-oriented atmosphere might not seem a favorable context for long-term protests by victims, for example, of mercury poisoning in the areas. However, once the issue surfaced, and their injuries became life-threatening, these victims did begin to take action; and this could be viewed as an extremely radical act. The problem was presented in dramatic form to the entire society. A lawsuit concerning the Minamata mercury-poisoning incident was filed in 1966, but the types of direct action carried out in a variety of contexts by the local citizens' movements, such as sit-ins directed at industries or city councils, attracted most of the attention. Given the conservatism of the rural setting, it was not individuals or groups in the area that gave them most of their support, but mainly politically radical scientists in the cities. Fortunately, the problem clearly showed the counterproductive side of economic growth and contributed to a universal critique of growth-first policies.

The preventive, urban type of movement continued through the 1970s. Perhaps because of the continuation of rapid economic growth, the middle class—in its consciousness and in its material base—had spread throughout the nation, and the urban type of citizens' consciousness extended even to these areas. Beginning in 1960, the urban type of citizens' consciousness matured. Murakami Yasusuke (1985) calls this the "new middle class," or "the new middle mass." The critical tendency of the new middle mass appeared first in the outpouring of local citizens' movements and leftist local governments, but from the late 1970s on, in the midst of a worldwide economic recession, they began to vote for conservative candidates because of their anxiety over economic problems (Inoguchi 1983: chap. 7; Miyake et al. 1985: 301–5).

"Leftist" Local Governments. An increase in leftist governments is one more important characteristic of local political changes in the postwar period. The term *leftist governments* refers to cases where the local executive is elected with the support of the Japan Socialist Party or the Japan Communist Party, or both. Ideologically these governments are clearly linked to the national-level political opposition. In 1964, when the League of Progressive Mayors organized, it had about 10 participants. By 1974 the number had grown to about 140 out of 600. At that time, Tokyo, Osaka, Kyoto, and Saitama prefectures had progressive governments in the sense discussed above, as did the large cities of Osaka, Kyoto, Yokohama, Nagoya, Kawasaki, and Kobe. Their "progressivization" entailed a number of problems that call for explanation; here, I will simply summarize a few points regarding the process.

First, the appearance of progressive governments broke down regional conditions that had been frozen in consensus for a long time, and internal conflicts emerged. Even where the executive was leftist, almost all leftist governments had legislatures with conservative majorities. Often policy proposals from the executives concerning "political" issues were rejected. For example, in the city of Kawasaki in 1972, a tree-planting plan was submitted to the city council by the mayor, an environmentalist, and in 1973, a city charter was proposed. They were both rejected. Even when there was no conflict over the content of policies, opposition-led city councils often confronted the executives in the city government and made full use of the councils' power to approve personnel decisions. It was easy for the appointment or dismissal of lieutenant governors, assistants, and members of education and public safety boards to become points of political contention. In the case of Yokohama, the plan submitted by Mayor Asukata for a "conference of ten thousand" was stymied because of the opposition of the city council (Sankei Shinbun Chihō Jichi Shuzaihan 1973: 49–53).

Second, the progressive governments brought with them a new political-administrative style of contact with the residents of the city. Asukata's "conference of ten thousand" and Tokyo Governor Minobe's "dialogue with citizens" are concrete examples of approaches that brought a freshness to these contacts. Clearly, these slogans enhanced a mood in city administration that responded to demands for participation. One cannot say they substantially closed the gap between the administration and the residents (see, for example, the discussion of the Tokyo "garbage war" in Yorimoto 1974). But they did emphasize official reports and public relations, compensating for the political loss of "direct ties to the center" with "direct ties to the citizens." ,

Third, there was a change in what we earlier called the "usual form" of decision making. It became difficult for the LDP to win election to executive positions in urban areas. The pattern of the gubernatorial elections in Kyoto (1970), Tokyo (1971), and Osaka (1971) gave people this impression. Beginning in the late 1970s, the conservatives recaptured the governor's seats in these three areas, but the unpredictability of city elections increased—for all sides. And competitiveness also increased in the election of local executives. As a result, paradoxical as it may seem, beginning in the late 1970s in the mayoralty elections of large cities such as Kyoto, Osaka, and Kobe, winning candidates appeared who were supported or nominated by an alliance of both ruling and opposition parties, or even by every party from the LDP to the Communists (Sasaki 1985: 217). One reason the opposition parties came aboard was because they lacked votes individually, but in addition, once they had tasted power, they could not forget its flavor. Because of these five-party nominations, elections sometimes became meaningless and the administration of local government tended to weaken.

Fourth, politically, the union of government administration and citizen participation opened up the possibility of excluding "politics" (here local legislature) by legitimizing the administration, while creating a different kind of power. Local leftist governments succeeded in generating new methods for dealing with pollution and social welfare within Japan's pluralistic political system. In Japan, the administrative process has traditionally been inhospitable to politics (i.e., the legislature). Because for a long time "modernization" was the clear goal, politics may have been seen as an obstacle that could be dispensed with. At both the national and the local levels, the bureaucracy lay at the core of the preparation of policy proposals, deliberation in the legislature, and the process of implementation. At the local level, because of the agency-delegated functions, which constituted 70 to 80 percent of the administrative tasks, it was said that the power of local legislatures to decide was small; they were given nothing more than the weak power of interpellation. And this tendency to minimize the scope of politics surfaced again when procedures for participation in mayoral decisions were established in response to an increase in participation.

The city of Yokohama was one of the first to establish direct dialogue with its residents. The mayor used a "conference of ten thousand," "consultations with citizens," and citizens councils in every ward, processes that were asserted to be direct democracy by Asukata (1965) and his followers. Clearly, this direct method was intended to circumvent the legislative bodies, where conservatives were dominant, and local power structures. When the administration established direct relations with the citizens, it became easier to bypass the legislatures, which reacted with hostility.

In 1970 the city of Kobe began to revise its master plan. A master plan advisory commission was founded in July 1974. The task given to the commission was to transform the development-oriented plan of 1966 into a human-centered plan. When the master plan was about to be adopted, the administration circumvented a recent (1969) revision of the local government law (Article 2, Section 5), which required city council's consent to the plan, by going to the citizens before the council's deliberations. Administrative officials met citizens in seventy-five places with a total of 4,943 participants. In this way the administration and the people had combined forces, and it was difficult for the council to take issue with a proposal created from citizens' opinions.

Fifth, citizen participation had an influence on central-local relations—a point I will discuss in the next section.

The Shared (or Fused) System and Leftist Local Government. The central ministries in Japan exercise tutelary supervision over local governments. Not only through agency-delegated functions but also through a variety of subsidy projects, the ministries realize their own plans in local areas. Of course, even in these cases, local governments have both *de facto* and *de jure* freedom and discretion to make rational choices to pick up any agency slack. In such cases, administrative functions are "shared" by the central and the local governments. Since the distribution of the regional transfer tax corresponds to local financial needs, which change every year, the amount of money distributed changes little by little. The Ministry of Home Affairs, which controls the transfer of the local distribution tax, exerts its influence by expressing its opinion of the activities and methods of local governments. It can be considered the central power in the shared system.

This system was originally adopted, in the words of Meiji-era leader Yamagata Aritomo, to "allow changes in the central political situation to reverberate in local governments" (quoted in Nagahama 1952), since the central bureaucracy was then engaged in bringing local administrations under its power and eliminating waste in the pursuit of rapid modernization. But conversely, as local citizens grew politically active in such a shared system, changes in local political situations can easily be transmitted to the center as well.

Agency-delegated functions are a typical part of the shared system. And usually policies reached through a natural agreement between the center and local governments, or vague "guidance" from the central bureaucracy, are adopted as local courses of action. But when local governments are not obedient partners, the central ministries find themselves in a crisis. When local governments agree with the claims of local citizens' movements and hold a view at odds with that of the central ministries, the ministries as senior partners are forced into the often uncomfortable position of making their attitudes clear. For example, in a Settsu lawsuit concerning the excessive burdens of nursery schools, the Ministry of Health and Welfare was forced to clarify its policy and philosophy toward nursery schools.

If we examine the spread of policy from local areas to the center and thence to the entire nation during the "age of progressive or leftist governments," it falls into three categories. First, some local governments' ideas directly influenced other local governments. Two examples are the agreements that were made between local governments and private industry to prevent pollution, and the residential land development guidance plans, which appeared first in the city of Kawanishi (Masago 1975). Generally, these measures can be divided into issues that clearly lay *within* the authority given by law to the local governments and those that clearly did not *contravene* their authority. Second, the policies of some local governments were centrally adopted as policies for the entire country. An example is free medical care for the elderly, which began in local areas and became national policy. Third, leftist governments sometimes chose political issues that would confront the central government, and these became national political issues. The municipalities' refusal to register military personnel as residents, and the semipublic election of school boards are two examples; the semipublic election of Tokyo ward heads is another important example. It is clear that in all three of these categories, leftist governments acted as levers. In this sense, they were very successful in introducing the reality of self-government into local politics, and the "usual" form of policy making began to change. I think that people use elections at the local level to criticize the central conservative government (Muramatsu 1975a). Rather than leaning strongly toward the Japan Socialist and Japan Communist Parties in national elections, they seem to find in local politics a way to criticize the one-party-dominant system, and accordingly place their support temporarily behind the left-wing opposition parties.

In this way, when citizens' movements in a shared system set local governments in motion, they can also press the central government to change its decisions. Then, whether the response of the central government is yes or no, the consequences of the response easily set a uniform standard throughout the country. Thus just as the earlier development-first mindset led to policy standards that controlled local governments all over the country, with the shift toward environmental values, these values quickly became the national standards. The shared system facilitated this mechanism. We can sense both its strengths and its weaknesses. The shared system enhanced the efficiency of local resistance and, as a result, unduly politicized the difference in opinion between the central and local governments; at the same time, in order to absorb the needs of local governments, the central government may have become overly accommodating.

From the Horizontal Political Competition Model to the Interdependent Relationship Model

Many scholars think that the typical pattern of the vertical administrative control model of the 1960s can be seen in the political processes surrounding the formation of the New Industrial City Construction Act in 1962 and the designation of new industrial cities under that law (e.g., Satō 1965; Ide 1972; Kawanaka 1967). Political scientists analyzed the processes by examining cross sections of the vertical administration. In the legislative process at the center, the turf wars of the central ministries (Transport; International Trade and Industry; Home Affairs; Agriculture, Forestry, and Fisheries; Construction) were fierce; because these vertical splits became obvious in local policy decisions about regional development based on the 1962 act, attention focused directly on the vertical administration. And because the guidance from each ministry was vertically compartmentalized, the governors were probably correct in feeling that it was difficult to coordinate matters across the departments at the prefecture level. The planning capabilities of the prefectures were as yet insufficiently developed (Ide 1972: 55–56), and their assemblies were powerless and tended to follow along in the wake of executive proposals. In sum, issues surrounding the new industrial cities came to be interpreted "administratively."

It is not that political considerations are completely missing from research on the new industrial city issue. Ide Yoshinori (1972) is aware of politicians' participation in the designating process, and of local movements. But in his study, he evaluates the former as peripheral and the latter as nothing more than trivial regional egoism. Consequently, he records the interventions in central LDP policy formation when local governments used their local Diet members to mobilize "the greatest petition war in history," but he does not adequately connect them theoretically. Specifically, these political elements are recorded because they stand out in the process of observation, but they are used as only peripheral or insignificant explanatory components of the vertical administrative control model. I would like to provide a unified explanation for these apparently scattered activities.

I think the essence of a new model lies in elections. And mayoral elections typify the structure of elections at all levels. It is in mayoral elections that the political forces of a locality engage in debate about the ideal shape of local society. No matter what kind of local government is elected, in order to realize its course of action under the present administrative, political, and financial structure, it must have the cooperation of the central government. Thus, each local government engages in activities that pressure or petition the center. Here a space arises in which local Diet members can work. In the case of the new industrial cities, the petition war was carried out with Diet members in the vanguard. The prefectures became the nucleus of lobbying activity directed toward the central government, but because the points at issue were also related to the fate of the municipalities, the prefectures communicated and coordinated their efforts closely with them. In this sense, local governments created powerful lobbying alliances, and Diet members could play the role of local representative to their hearts' content. Nevertheless, what seems remarkable in the activities of the Diet members is their focus on the policy-making process. Although the new industrial city plan was prepared and presented by the economic agencies of the bureaucracy, the LDP strongly intervened on two points.

First, the original plan intended to concentrate investment in just a few places, targeting the Pacific Coast (especially the Tokaidodo region), thus promoting efficient economic investment. But in response, the LDP intervened. First, as I have already described, the agricultural lobby within the LDP opposed the fixation of the bureaucracy on economic efficiency and formed an agricultural friendship society. In the formulation of the Comprehensive National Development Plan, which became the basis for the concept of new industrial cities, they pushed "the correction of income discrepancy" between cities and the agricultural villages to the fore, bringing about a revision of the basic goals of the Zenso (Masumi 1969: 409–10). Before the appeals for specific designations were made—that is, before the New Industrial City Construction Act was put into effect—the Diet members worked for their localities during the planning stages. Second, there was a jurisdictional fight among several agencies over the new industrial cities plan, and a total of six ministries—International Trade and Industry; Agriculture, Forestry, and Fisheries; Home Affairs; Construction; Transport; and Labor—put forth their own plans for local development. Voluntary coordination among the ministries and agencies was impossible. Finally, the Policy Affairs Research Council of the LDP entered the picture and brought about a compromise, making the Economic Planning Agency the mediator of the whole operation. Clearly, this shows that at the policy-formation stage, the political party set the course.

Because politics at the central and local levels are interlocking, they determine the quality of central-local relations overall. The character of this linkage can be explained partly in terms of administrative relationships and partly in terms of party activities and elections. My own emphasis expands the aspect in which the lobbying activities and rivalries that boil up from the bottom determine central-local relations. The way the horizontal political competition model applies to environmental problems and welfare policies differs from the way it applies to the new industrial cities. Specifically, when some local governments adopted policies in the former fields, they promptly spread to other local governments, but the means of their expansion was not downward impetus from the administration; rather, it came from lateral rivalries stimulated by politics and elections.

With both environmental and welfare policies, the local governments that adopted them had an oppositional relationship with the related ministries and agencies that differed from that of the past. In Kumamoto prefecture, which Steven Reed (1979) has studied, the local government had fierce exchanges with the Ministry of International Trade and Industry (MITI) over environmental standards. Even though it expected this situation, the local government was forced into responding because other local governments were responding to the demands of their citizens. Horizontal competition is intense. And when the actions of individual local governments are coordinated, the process has an impact on the policies of central ministries and agencies. Such policies then may spread even more quickly if the central government adopts them. Free medical care for the elderly is a case in point.

The reason that I call this competition "horizontal" is that the competition among local areas stands out. It is also "political," because this competitive process is based on elections.

In the case of Japan, even amid the rivalry among local areas, what is distinctive is its horizontal nature, involving localities of similar size. Here I mean that every local government acts so as not to fall behind, or even at times to outstrip, the policy standards of the local governments it considers its rivals. There are two kinds of horizontal competition that take as their standard rival local governments. First, there are lateral orientations among neighboring local governments. It is easy to disseminate the policy standards or techniques of local governments to their surrounding areas. Moreover, neighboring local governments that possess a sense of unity tend to create arenas for the exchange of various kinds of information and to exchange opinions. The Osaka-Kobe Regional Cities Council and the three suburbs of Kyoto known as the "Two Cities, One Town" (the cities of Nagaokakyo and Muko and the town of Oyamazaki) have become these kinds of units of information exchange.

The other form of horizontal competition can be seen among local governments with similar characteristics. Formerly, Osaka and Tokyo, Kobe (Kansai area) and Yokohama (Tokyo area), and Amagasaki (Kansai area) and Kawasaki (Tokyo area) compared administrative standards on the assumption that they had similar characteristics and patterns (although the Kansai cities in these pairs have since become smaller in their scale and functions than corresponding cities in the Tokyo area). I could add that in a 1981 study I conducted of leading administrators of Kyoto, one of the then-ten designated cities, when I asked where they looked for standards for their own decisions, the majority replied "to the other designated cities" (Miyake and Muramatsu 1981: 459–60).

Rivalry for lateral status can arise in the vertical administrative control model as well, as pointed out in Ōmori Wataru and Satō Seizaburō

(1986). I agree, but I am also trying to understand lateral status by linking it with the election mechanism. As I discussed above, the political
competition model serves this purpose. I think that the political will of a
local community, which is exhibited mainly in elections, is a powerful
impulse in the central-local relations of postwar Japan. Therefore, when
the drive to maintain lateral status combines with political will, it is very
difficult to suppress the political dynamism thus generated. In this sense,
the consciousness of lateral status is an important element in forming my
horizontal political competition model. In cases where policies have
been presented as public commitments in order to appeal to the citizens;
in cases where, even without making a public commitment, policies
have been presented laterally in order to appeal to support groups or
voters; and even in cases of central ministries and prefectural guidance
and legal, financial, and structural limits—in all these cases, it is emi-
nently possible for local policy makers to go to the limits of their powers, or even to cross over these limits and move into the implementation
of policy. In cases where implementation is demanded by a powerful
local group, this tendency becomes even clearer. From the late 1960s to
the early 1970s, a policy was put into effect that raised the salaries across
the board for local officials in the Tokyo and Osaka metropolitan areas.
Its implementation over the resistance of the central leadership is an example of one form of horizontal competition. In this case, the focus was
the local officials' associations.

Here, let me outline the new horizontal political competition model
I have just presented.

First, in this model, the political actors are governments at the central
and the local levels—combinations of local governments, individual
politicians, administrators, pressure groups, influential individuals, and
the like—all political actors conceivable. But the local level must be
thought of as divided between prefectures and municipalities. There are
inevitably differences between government strategies at the municipal
and the prefectural levels.

Second, the success of local government strategy depends on the
number of political resources an area has and its skill in using them. This
presupposes considerable room for independent activity in the local
areas. In the previous model, analysis considered only legal authority
and procedures as political resources or rules. It suggested that local governments had little room to maneuver, and critically analyzed Japan's
legally centralized structure from a pro-local autonomy perspective. In
its view, what stood at the core of this centralized structure and gave or-

ders to and restricted local governments was the bureaucratic system or the central ministries and agencies. But if we are clearly aware that different kinds of political resources or rules constitute the foundation of power, we realize that local governments have been abundantly endowed. Indeed, a special characteristic of contemporary society is the multiplicity of its political resources and their wide dispersion. The question is how these resources are used: influence must be analyzed first of all operationally. From this perspective, the opportunities for local influence created by the Japanese constitution and related local laws have not been sufficiently utilized. For example, in the case of excessive financial burdens on local governments, the governments can present claims to the ministers under Article 7 of the Local Finance Law. If the use of this procedure increases, the central government can be expected to take reactions into account *before* it takes action.

Third, the two models make different hypotheses about *where* the center and the local governments clash, negotiate, or compromise. In the vertical administrative control model, theoretically the location of central-local bargaining is the prefectural level. Clashes arise between bureaucrats from the center and local politicians such as governors or legislators. This is because high-ranking state officials are sent out as officials of prefectural governments in order to control the local politics that the governors and the legislators represent. But in the vertical administrative control model, gubernatorial leadership is negatively evaluated because conflict has tended to be resolved to the advantage of the central government. In contrast, in the horizontal political competition model, conflict arises at the center. At the local level, high-ranking centrally dispatched bureaucrats act as local bureaucrats. (Of course, they retain the attributes of central bureaucrats, but they minimize these aspects while they are in local government in order to perform the local positions they have been given.) The personal connections of these bureaucrats thus become political resources for the *local* areas. Therefore, the prefectures actually hope for the arrival from the center of capable bureaucrats with broad connections and persuasive powers vis-à-vis the central government. In any case, at the same time that the governors engage these bureaucrats and touch base with their local Diet members, they go off to Tokyo in order to pursue their goals. A careful analysis of this gubernatorial style of action is an important topic in this model.

Fourth, to borrow from neo-Marxist theory, the main theme of postwar Japanese local government has moved from "the accumulation of capital" to "public consumption." The functions shared by the central and the local governments have expanded in the process, and so have central-local relations themselves (Mizuguchi 1984). In presenting a new model for understanding Japanese central-local relations, I contend that the political aspect is important and horizontal political competition is needed, while keeping the orthodoxy of vertical control. Historically, we see that gradually politics has succeeded in penetrating into the administration-dominated central-local relationship. In order to analyze this kind of situation, we need another model (here the interdependent relationship model) in which central and local initiatives are mutually accepted and the officials of both governments interact intensively to produce public policies. The cooperation between the two levels of governments takes many forms. Often the central ministries propose new programs and place them in the framework of agency delegation. In this way the central ministry has a final say in the process of implementation, even with regard to the detailed parts of the policies delegated to localities. On the other hand, localities frequently express their views in carrying out the various programs under the framework of central supervision and enter into conflict with the central ministries.

CHAPTER 3

The Changing Role
of the Prefectures

An Analysis of Gubernatorial Interview Data

In order to demonstrate the effectiveness of this new explanatory model of central-local relations, we must substantiate it with data. One method is to focus on specific administrative functions and conduct case studies of how the national, prefectural, and municipal governments perform them. After completing the case studies, we could then make some generalizations. We can also obtain supporting data by gathering together studies of local officials or agency-delegated functions, or from a reanalysis of the key decisions (Dahl 1957) that previous local government research has revealed. In chapter 2, for example, I reanalyzed or reinterpreted existing research data pertaining to regional policies and local development from my own view.

Another method is to survey national, prefectural, and municipal officials and, through statistical analysis of the data, to identify the patterns of exchanges among them. By preparing careful hypotheses about conflict and cooperation between politics and administration and the power relations among the three levels of government, we can obtain abundant information about Japan's intergovernmental relations and will also be able to generalize to a considerable degree about the characteristics of the prefectures as an intermediate body.

Taking up the second method first, I would like to discuss the character of the prefectures and the form of Japan's central-local relations. But with only gubernatorial interview data as its base, this book is not the systematic type of investigation called for above. Even if we are able to discover new perspectives from it, what it can directly demonstrate is limited. But if we link this new perspective on Japanese central-local relations with information obtained from reinterpretation of the existing data to the political system as a whole, I think we have the opportunity to discover a new role for local government.

There is a reason for being interested in the opinions and actions of the prefectural governors. In the postwar period the greatest concern of the bureaucrats, living within the traditions of the former Home Ministry, has been keeping governors under their control by means of agency-delegated functions (Akagi 1978: pt. 1, chap. 2; Takagi 1974: 259–63). Therefore, let us first consider the institutional development of the prefectures.

The Prewar Prefecture System: Agents of the National Government

The prefectures are intermediate bodies, standing between the state and the municipalities. What does that mean? Put simply, while linked to the national government, they advise the municipalities on interpretations of the law and oversee local finances, and they function as agents to the municipalities in various national undertakings, as well as agents to the national government in municipal undertakings. What should be noted is that today, in their position in the middle, the prefectures also initiate their own operations, and to execute them, they interact and negotiate with both the national government and the municipalities. But, to go beyond this kind of abstract discussion, we must trace the development of the prefectures in order to discover their political character.

The prefectural system of today can be traced to the end of the Tokugawa-era feudal domains and the establishment of the prefectures. In July 1871 the feudal domains of the Tokugawa period were abolished by imperial decree; the system of prefectures that replaced them emphasized the unity of domestic politics. The previous local government structure had been a transitional measure in the move away from the old Tokugawa regime. But the prefectural system of 1871 was also an unstable mechanism; it was only a step toward the system finally established in 1890. Still, it was an important measure that determined the later intermediate position of the prefectures. The major functions of the new prefectural administrations were the supervision of (1) the actions of municipal offices established below it; (2) lawsuits, public order, judicial affairs, and tax collection within the prefecture; and (3) fiscal transfers to the Ministry of Finance (Rekidai Chiji Hensankai 1981: 22). In this period, legal institutions at the municipal level were in flux, as were the authority and scale of institutions at the prefectural level. It seems that no one had yet sufficiently grasped what to do about political administration at the prefectural level, or how to do it.

With regard to scale, the system originally arranged the prefectures into 3 *fu* and 302 *ken*, which later became 2 *fu* and 72 *ken*. They were stabilized at 3 *fu* and 43 *ken* in the prefecture system of 1890. Their authority and functions also seem to have stabilized between 1888 and 1890. The prefectures were originally the relay points for all national functions, but after 1872 judicial functions were transferred to the judicial system (with its newly established courts) and thus the prefectures' functions were limited to those of administration in the executive branch. The reallocation of functions that continued into the postwar period began in 1871 with the assignment of family registration (the keeping of family background records for all residents) to the municipalities: the municipalities—which were in direct contact with their residents—conducted business on the front line, and the prefectures took on supervisory functions. It is likely that this reduction in the power of the prefectures was planned to correspond with an increase in the size of the municipalities: under a program of consolidation urged by the central government, the 71,498 cities, towns, and villages of 1869 had by 1889 decreased to 15,859.

The size of the prefectures was also related to the size of the *gun*, or counties. As units located between the prefectures and the municipalities, *gun* were an imported concept, modeled on the Prussian *Kreis*; they were established in 1889 after the institution of the Three New Laws (Steiner 1965: 30–32). Their role was to settle, on the spot but against a background of national aims, problems that could not be settled within the framework of the municipalities. Young state bureaucrats were appointed as *gun* chiefs. But in the 1910s and 1920s the reasons for their existence came into question—in part because they lacked the traditional social and economic base of the *Kreis*; in part because the scale of the basic governmental units had been enlarged by the consolidation of the cities, towns, and villages; and more directly, because the *gun* system could not cope with repeated tenant disputes.

Against this background, and in order to move democratization one step further from state restraints, the *gun* system was brought to an end in 1921; the *gun* government offices were abolished in 1926. (For the dynamics of the abolition of the *gun,* see Mitani 1967: 70–132. Today, *gun* have no real substance except as postal addresses or election district boundaries; still, they can be important in considering regional limits — for example, when the old boundaries of a county become the limits of a newly created municipality.)

In this way, Japan's central-local relations acquired three levels: national, prefectural, and municipal. The prefectures absorbed the former supervisory functions of the *gun* and were refined into units that supervised the municipalities as agents of state will. The prefectures had two departments: police and home affairs. Eventually some of the functions of the Department of Home Affairs were moved to the newly established Department of Social Affairs. Then, as society grew more complex, a number of specialized offices were established that were not included in these three departments.

Changes are also visible in the jurisdiction of the prefectural assemblies. The assemblies were first officially recognized when the Three New Laws systematized the deliberative organizations that had already existed in a number of areas. Then came the prefecture system of 1890, under which, after the experience of the Three New Laws period, the authority of the assemblies was gradually reduced. Furthermore, the previous right of the prefectural assemblies to propose legislation was given to the governors. And in order to make it impossible for the assemblies to resist the will of the central government, the home minister was given the authority to dissolve them.

The governors were government appointees; the power to appoint and dismiss governors was given to the home minister. Most important, the legal system relating to the appointment of governors was based on an imperial edict (Article 10 of the Meiji Constitution), which did not entail any input from the Imperial Diet. This system, the local government organization system, was intended to minimize the activities of the political parties and particularly the influence of protest or opposition movements on the administration of government policy.

After 1888 the municipalities were granted considerable autonomy. Generally, the mayors and legislators of towns and villages were chosen by election. First, citizens who were qualified to vote chose the town or village assembly; then the mayor was elected indirectly, by the assembly. In contrast, cities were to some degree under the control of the central government: the election of city council members was the same as in the towns and villages, but the mayor was appointed by the home minister from among three candidates selected by the city council. In addition, state law established executive secretariats (composed of mayors, deputy mayors, and senior council members) in the cities. The three major cities of Tokyo, Kyoto, and Osaka had mayors, but their mayors were concurrently governors—appointed in Tokyo—of the prefectures in which these cities were located. Therefore, local autonomy was weak. Nevertheless, it was these three cities that had the highest capacity for autonomy, and they repeatedly resisted the state control that came through the prefectures. The movement for expansion of their autonomy, as seen in the debate over the "special cities" issue of the 1940s and 1950s, lasted clear into the postwar period. (In the "special cities" issue, five major cities, including Osaka and Kyoto, demanded to raise their legal status to equal that of the prefectures, as discussed in chapter 1, but their efforts failed.)

This institutional framework is usually described as a completely centralized system. But its actual administration was more complex than it appears. Taking the case of a historian's study (Ariizumi 1980) of Yamanashi prefecture, we find that local areas had both the initiative and the determination needed to solve local problems. We must therefore temper the centralization arguments of the old institutional theorists. First, it seems that the conventional picture is slightly exaggerated. For example, ten years after the establishment of the prefectural system, that system was not yet in effect in seven prefectures. In addition, town and village assemblies were often destabilized by political controversies surrounding the election of *gun* or prefectural legislators. And the governors, who as the nucleus of intergovernmental relations were supposed to stabilize the whole governmental system, also became embroiled in political conflict. These facts have not been taken into account in the orthodox theories of the past.

Indeed, the following kind of situation was not unusual, according to specialists in the prewar period: "Because the influence of the political parties permeated local government, local party power affected not only local personnel but also roads, public works, and railroad and school construction, which became the tools of party interests and stratagems. . . . In prefectures like Ōita, Kumamoto, Saga, Ishikawa, and Akita political conflict was especially fierce; for example, even the inns belonged to either the Seiyū faction or the Minsei political faction, and even police patrolmen were transferred every time the government changed" (Rekidai Chiji Hensankai 1981: 52). The text following this passage states that "the invasion of party influence . . . brought about many abuses" not only in the prefectural governments but also in "local governments" (probably meaning the municipalities). How can a strict application of the centralization model, as in the past, incorporate this kind of situation?

I think we need a theory of prewar central-local relations that includes a balance of the types of specific phenomena described above. Still, when we compare them with postwar phenomena, prewar central-local relations do seem to be controlled by the center, with the prefectures acting as its agents. The mechanism that assigned the resolution of major problems to the central government was built into the political structure; moreover, it was often activated. The possibility of creating a more centrally concentrated authority structure was pursued in the period from 1940 to 1945, with the establishment of a new revenue equalization system for localities (1940), the creation of a unified metropolitan government in Tokyo, the legalization of neighborhood associations (1940), and the creation of a regional system in which regional governors (concurrently the governor of one of the prefectures in the region) served to oversee wartime administration and mobilization (1944). Local governments were truly reduced to the lowest stratum of the state during this period. This experience has survived in the form of a hostility lying beneath the surface of scholars' orthodox theories of local government in the postwar period. But a flexible understanding of the prewar system of concentrated power is important to a full understanding of the postwar period.

Accordingly, prewar central-local relations can be summarized as follows:

1. The prefectures were the agents of the state. The governors represented the nation as a whole at the local level. In contrast, the municipalities and prefectural assemblies to some extent were constructed to reflect the local will.

2. There were periods when electoral and party politics were active, and prefectural administrative structures could not avoid being affected, but ultimately the system was able to contain these effects. Politics, which became active in specific periods, gradually receded each time, and as the war expanded, the authority of the governors came to dominate local governments.

3. Although not detailed above, the "moral hegemony" (Tarrow 1977: chap. 1) of the central bureaucratic system, which derived from its responsibility for spearheading Japan's modernization, enhanced

the power of an administrative structure based on it and the governors. The national goal of achieving modernization and the aura of the emperor lay at the disposal of the state and the bureaucratic system. But moral hegemony inevitably would decline as the goal of modernization was achieved, with the results we shall see below.

The Postwar Prefecture System: Intermediate Bodies

Let us look at Takagi Shōsaku's analysis of the characteristics of postwar prefectures as intermediate bodies (1979: 2–4). Takagi attributes to these bodies a dual meaning. First, they are intermediate because of their "prefectural characteristics": the prefectures are local governments, but compared with the "purely" local self-governing bodies, the municipalities, they are tinged with characteristics of the state. These state characteristics are manifested in the many agency-delegated functions imposed by the central government. Second, they are intermediate because their "managerial capacities" lie between those of the national government and the municipalities. Takagi does not discuss these capacities in detail, but in general he means administrative, financial, and political capacities, which include the scale of financial resources and specialized knowledge. What deserves attention is Takagi's suggestion that the emphasis on prefectures' role as intermediate bodies has moved from the first sense of the term to the second. As Takagi observes, prefectures have decreased their function to mediate state policies to municipalities. Nowadays, they take initiative in raising projects suitable to their capacities, a middle range of projects.

To add my own interpretation, Takagi's first sense applies particularly to the period from 1945 to 1955. At this time the central ministries and agencies constantly restrained the prefectures and their governors so that they would act as their agents. When the postwar constitution was written, the bureaucrats resolved to push for the direct election of governors because they foresaw that the will of the central government could be imposed locally by widely adopting the system of agency-delegated functions (Akagi 1978: 28–29). But even so, the ministries and agencies' anxieties continued, so they strengthened their local branch offices.

The Fourth Advisory Council on the Local Government System (1955) is famous for its report on the "regional" (or *dōshū*) system. Its report proposed both a return to appointed governors and a plan to abolish the prefectures, consolidating them into regions. In the proposed regional system, the heads of regional governments were to be appointed by the prime minister, contingent on the approval of directly elected legislatures. The proposals were not adopted, and afterward plans for abolishing the prefectures and for the appointment of governors seemed to have disappeared from the discussions of the council. However, the issue of broad regionalization continued in the form of a plan to consolidate the three Pacific Coast prefectures and one to consolidate Osaka, Nara, and Wakayama prefectures; a prefectural consolidation plan was put forward by the Tenth Advisory Council on the Local Government System (1965), followed by a regional agency plan from the First Provisional Administrative Reform Commission (1962) and another *dōshū* proposal from the Japan Chamber of Commerce and Industry (1970). The Kansai business community was especially supportive of the *dōshū* system and consolidation of the prefectures, with an eye to the efficient use of water resources. Discussions of such issues within the central government were replete with references to "the untrustworthiness of local government," and the freedom of action of the governors was subsequently restrained.

In the process of achieving systemic stability, in addition to this "restraint from above," the prefectures were "restrained from below" by the "special cities" issue discussed above. This system resulted from a successful movement by the five major cities (Osaka, Kyoto, Nagoya, Kobe, and Yokohama): when the postwar local government law was enacted, the special municipality system was written into it as Articles 264–80. The issue of the special municipality system was finally concluded with the compromise of 1957, which transferred sixteen prefectural functions to these cities.

The second period posited by Takagi is distinguished by the prefectures' beginning to carry out independent activities after the late 1960s. Broadly speaking, this was a period when the prefectures were liberated from state restraints and began to pursue the possibilities inherently guaranteed in their legal structure as local governments. Regional development, environmental administration, welfare policies—these are all concrete examples of the new activities of this period. In these activities, the prefectures expanded into a variety of new relationships with both the central government and the municipalities. With both these and their more traditional functions, the prefectures discovered a larger role than they had had before, not only in communicating the purposes of the central government to the municipalities, but also in transmitting the intentions of the municipalities or their own opinions or demands to the central government. In the first period, the structure of the relationship among the three parties was state and prefectures *versus* municipalities. In the second, the prefectures responded confrontationally and cooperatively to both the central government and the municipalities and did not necessarily act consistently as the partner of either side. It was during this period that Liberal Democratic Party dominance was established, and the movement of authority from the bureaucracy to the party also influenced the prefectures' modes of activity. Extending Takagi's analysis, we can describe the more recent relationship of the three levels, in the 1980s, as the state versus the prefectures and municipalities. Although the municipal interests are more saliently expressed vis-à-vis the prefectures in the policy process, there is no doubt that the prefectures follow the logic of electoral politics rather than that of bureaucratic politics at the center.

An Analysis of the Data

Finally, we come to the gubernatorial interview data, but first let me review the new theory that these data will substantiate. This theory tries to comprehend Japan's postwar central-local relations in terms of overlapping authority or shared authority. This model does not ignore the control of localities by the state, which the old vertical administrative control model emphasized. On the one hand, it recognizes the existence of administrative control of local governments by the center. On the other hand, it suggests that even within such control, and in the broader political context, the center also depends on the local governments; therefore, local governments can exert influence over the state. In other words, it tries to integrate both those aspects into a single model. In contrast to existing theory, which focuses exclusively on the control of localities by the center, this perspective notes that local governments have autonomous purposes and that they put pressure on the central government in order to realize them. The prefectures are intermediate bodies that mediate this control, dependence, and influence between the center and the municipalities. The direct guarantees of this system are found in the Japanese constitution (Article 8, which pertains to local government) and the Local Government Act.

Essentially, the postwar constitution and the Local Government Act established the framework for a new, decentralized central-local relationship by providing for the direct popular election of governors. My focus here is on whether, as a result of direct election, the prefectures' character as intermediate bodies has changed from being agents of the state to serving as intermediaries for both sides, and specifically on what form this change may have taken. Revising the previous image, I propose that the situation is becoming one of the center *versus* the prefectures and municipalities. I would like to call this interpretation, which sees intergovernmental relations as a bilateral relationship, the "overlapping or shared authority relationship" model. In the pages that follow I will use the gubernatorial interview data to see to what degree relationships of overlapping authority can be verified.

Note: The gubernatorial survey was conducted from April to June 1981. The researchers were members of the Political Science Research Group of the Kyoto University Law School, and the actual interviews were carried out by the Central Opinion Research Company (Chūō Chōsa Sha). Out of forty-seven governors, four were ill or could not be interviewed during the prescribed period because of time constraints. The division below of the forty-three governors into urban, quasi-urban, and rural areas is based on the proportion of the prefectural workforce in primary industry. The prefectures in each category are as follows:

Urban: Saitama, Tokyo, Kanagawa, Gifu, Shizuoka, Aichi, Kyōto, Ōsaka, Hyōgo, Nara, Fukushima.

Quasi-urban: Hokkaidō, Miyagi, Tochigi, Gunma, Chiba, Toyama, Ishikawa, Fukui, Yamanashi, Mie, Shiga, Wakayama, Okayama, Yamaguchi, Kagawa, Ehime, Okinawa.

Rural: Aomori, Iwate, Yamagata, Fukushima, Niigata, Nagano, Tottori, Shimane, Tokushima, Kōchi, Saga, Kumamoto, Ōita, Miyazaki, Kagoshima.

THE ROLE OF THE PREFECTURES

First, let us present the responses of the prefectural governors to the question "What is the role of the governor?" When given two choices—"To execute national policy within the prefecture" or "To work toward national policies that address local problems"—the overwhelming majority (98 percent) chose the latter (table 3). Below, as we consider

Table 3 *Which Activity Should Governors Emphasize?*

Activity	Responses (%)[a]
Execute national policy within the prefecture	2
Work toward national policies that address local problems	98

[a] "Other" responses have been omitted.

other, more detailed analysis of their authority, we should keep in mind that they solidly presuppose this latter role of the governor. Although their legal authority still retains statist characteristics, the governors' consciousness reflects the fact that the prefectures are becoming powerful regional advocates. This basic attitude shapes the other aspects of the governors' perception of intergovernmental relations.

PERCEPTIONS OF AUTHORITY

Table 4 shows the responses to the question of whether the authority delegated to the prefectures in their relations with both the national government and the municipalities is adequate. The governors replied that their authority in relation to the national government was "insufficient"; in relation to the municipalities, it was "just right" or "excessive." Here, there is a clear recognition of their intermediate power position. The governors feel the pressure of the state; accordingly, as those responsible for local government, they were critical of their inadequate position in the national power structure.

Similar information can be obtained from data about differences of opinion (which can also be interpreted as confrontations). As shown in table 5, the governors thought there were many such differences with the central government, but almost none with the municipalities. There are a number of ways to interpret this. Perhaps the municipalities are persuaded by the prefectures, so confrontation is not felt. But the prefectures have many clear differences of opinion with the national government. Or perhaps it is that, psychologically, differences of opinion with the national government make a large impression on the governors, but differences with the municipalities do not. Indeed, from a systemic perspective, we can surmise that the responses reflect the fact that many conflicts with the municipalities are not even recognized by the governors. The governor rarely takes part in negotiations with the municipalities, which must be entrusted to subordinates. In contrast, the governor

Table 4 *Prefectural Authority*

	Degree of Prefectural Authority (%)[a]				
	Excessive	*Just Right*	*Insufficient*	*No Answer*	*N*
In relation to central government	—	16	79	5	43
In relation to municipalities	37	51	12	0	43

QUESTIONS: First, what do you think about the present authority of your prefecture in relation to the central government?

Second, what about the present authority of your prefecture in relation to that of the municipalities?

[a]In this and all subsequent tables 100% of the responses are accounted for, although the figures have been rounded off.

Table 5 *Opposition between Prefectures and Other Levels of Government*

	Differences with Other Levels (%)						
	Very Many	*Many*	*Some*	*A Few*	*Very Few*	*No Answer*	*N*
With central government	5	26	35	21	17	2	43
With municipalities	0	5	28	30	37	0	43

QUESTIONS: During the past three years, how many differences of opinion or interest did your prefecture have with the central government? Please include cases where the differences were small or where they were subsequently resolved.

What about differences with the municipalities? Please give your general impression of the differences of opinion or interest your prefecture had with the municipalities during the past three years.

Table 6 *Prefectural Authority in Relation to Central Government by Type of Prefecture*

	Prefectural Authority (%)				
Type of Prefecture	*Excessive*	*Just Right*	*Insufficient*	*No Answer*	*N*
Rural	0	20	73	7	15
Quasi-urban	0	18	77	6	17
Urban	0	9	91	—	11

Table 7 *Prefectural Confrontation with Central Government by Type of Prefecture*

Type of Prefecture	Frequency of Confrontation (%)			
	Often or Somewhat Often	*Occasional*	*Somewhat Rare or Rare*[a]	*N*
Rural	34	33	33	15
Quasi-urban	24	35	42	17
Urban	36	36	27	11

[a] "No answer" was interpreted as a negative opinion or explanation and included in this category.

himself ordinarily takes the lead in handling differences of opinion or conflicts with the national government.

Going further, let us divide the governors into urban, quasi-urban, and rural prefectures, and analyze their differences of opinion over authority and confrontation. Tables 6 and 7 indicate their perceptions of their relations with the national government. Governors of urban areas were especially likely to say that their authority vis-à-vis the central government was insufficient. There was comparatively less dissatisfaction among governors of quasi-urban and rural prefectures, although more than 70 percent did voice discontent. The governors of urban areas also perceived a large number of confrontations. But the patterns of response concerning confrontations and authority differ: one should note that governors of rural areas perceived an almost equally large number of confrontations.

What do we see when we compare the three groups' responses regarding authority and confrontation in relation to the municipalities? The data suggest that there was no overall dissatisfaction with the existing authority balance, but table 8 shows a particularly large number of "excessive" or "just right" responses from governors of quasi-urban areas. In contrast, among the urban and rural governors, about a fifth answered "insufficient." With regard to confrontation (table 9), nearly half the governors of urban areas responded "occasional," while the governors of quasi-urban and rural areas leaned more strongly toward "rare." As municipalities become urbanized, they promote their policies actively. As a result, these data may simply reflect the reality of increasing municipal activism rather than any conditions or psychological factors on the prefectural level.

Table 8 *Prefectural Authority in Relation to Municipalities by Type of Prefecture*

Type of Prefecture	Prefectural Authority (%)				
	Excessive	*Just Right*	*Insufficient*	*No Answer*	*N*
Rural	27	53	20	0	15
Quasi-urban	53	47	0	0	17
Urban	27	55	18	0	11

Table 9 *Prefectural Confrontation with Municipalities by Type of Prefecture*

Type of Prefecture	Frequency of Confrontation (%)			
	Often or Somewhat Often	*Occasional*	*Somewhat Rare or Rare*	*N*
Rural	0	27	73	15
Quasi-urban	6	18	77	17
Urban	9	46	46	11

THE CAUSES AND CONCILIATION
OF CONFLICT

Next, as we analyze the causes of conflict and its management (the success of efforts at persuasion or the success of opponents'
persuasion), let us clarify the strengths and weaknesses of intermediary
governments.

Let us compare the causes of prefectural confrontation with the central government and the municipalities. With the central government,
the primary cause was the uniformity of national policies, followed by
divergence of interests, and then by the center's insufficient consideration of financial conditions. With the municipalities, the governors said
that confrontations arose logically from the different interests of the prefecture and the municipalities. Although different interests were also important in conflicts with the national government, they were *relatively*
less so. With the municipalities, "different interests" were the number
one cause of conflict (cited by 79 percent of the governors); the second-
ranking reason for confrontation was the uniformity of prefectural policy, the third was financial reasons, and the fourth was differences in po-

Table 10 *Causes of Confrontation with Central Government and Municipalities*

	Causes (Total of 1st and 2d Responses)						
	Different Political Positions	Different Interests[a]	Policy Uniformity	Insufficient Financial Consideration	Other	No Answer[b]	N
Confrontation with central government	9	42	65	28	26	9 (30)	43
Confrontation with munici-palities	16	79	35	33	12	5 (25)	43

QUESTIONS: What do you think are the causes of differences in views or concerns between your prefecture and the national government (i.e., the central ministries)? From the following list of reasons, please select the two that are closest to your opinion and rank them in order of importance.

What about differences between your prefecture and the municipalities? Please select the two main ones from the following list of reasons and rank them in order of importance.

[a] In the case of the central government, "different interests" refers to differences between national and local interests; in the case of the municipalities, "different interests" refers to differences in the character of municipal interests and prefectural interests.

[b] The figures in parentheses are totals of all first and second "no answer" responses.

litical positions. As table 10 shows, divergent interests and political differences are much more characteristic causes of confrontation with the municipalities than with the central government, but this may indicate the governors' sensitivity toward the municipalities' partisan coloration (conservative, leftist, and the like).

The causes of conflict that the governors ranked first can be read in part as a justification for their own confrontational posture. They can say that the state makes conflict inevitable—the national government's lack of flexibility is overwhelmingly the justification. In contrast, in their relations with the municipalities under their supervision, it is as if prefectural interests simply made confrontations unavoidable. The governors ranked the rigid uniformity of prefectural policies second among causes of confrontations with the municipalities. Although this response is not a justification for the prefectures' actions, it seems to indicate the constraints on the prefectures within the national framework.

Let us move to an analysis of the reasons why persuasion succeeds in overcoming confrontation (table 11). Almost all the reasons given in table 11 seem to work less effectively in the governors' relations with the national government than in their relations with the municipalities. The

Table 11 *Reasons for Success of Persuasion*

	Reasons (Total of 1st, 2d, and 3d Responses)						
	Because of Legal Interpretation	*Appropriateness of the Policy Involved*	*Reliance on Revenue Performance*	*Support of Politicians*	*Other*	*No Answer[a]*	*N*
Persuasion of central government	16	84	23	49	49	12 (79)	43
Persuasion of municipalities	35	98	77	21	26	0 (43)	43

QUESTIONS: When your prefecture has been able to persuade the nation to do something, what do you think were the most effective reasons? Select three from the following list and rank them in order of importance.

Generally, the views and concerns of your prefecture and the municipalities in it are different, but when your prefecture has been able to persuade the municipalities to do something, what do you think were the main reasons? From the following list, select the three you think were most effective and rank them in order of importance.

[a]The figures in parentheses are the total number of "no answer" responses in each category.

governors thought that the appropriateness of their own policies and the fact that the municipalities depended on the revenue performance of the prefectures were especially linked to their success in persuading the municipalities. This finding agrees with R. A. W. Rhodes's (1982) hypothesis that, because all organizations do not possess all the resources they need, even the central government depends on the performance of local governments. Leadership through legal interpretation also seems to be more effective in relation to the municipalities. In contrast, the most striking characteristic of successful gubernatorial persuasion of the national government was the support of politicians. That is, in addition to the administrative route, there is a political route linking the governors and the state. In cases where the national government is the other player, this route becomes an effective ally of the prefectures. In instances where the municipalities make demands on the prefectures, the support of politicians is also effective. In contrast, politicians do not seem to involve themselves much when the central government imposes its will upon the prefectures. Still, the overall framework of central-local relations is on occasion determined by the political leadership.

Table 12 compares the governors' reasons for accepting persuasion by the national government and the municipalities. Many reasons were given for acquiescence to the municipalities: the first was appropriate policy (81 percent), the second was dependence on their performance,

Table 12 *Reasons for Being Persuaded*

	Reasons (Total of 1st, 2d, and 3d Responses)						
	Because of Legal Interpretation	*Appropriateness of the Policy Involved*	*Reliance on Revenue Performance*	*Support of Politicians*	*Other*	*No Answer*[a]	*N*
Persuasion by central government	26	42	30	7	30	28 (65)	43
Persuasion by municipalities	26	81	65	33	23	5 (72)	43

QUESTIONS: When your prefecture has had reasons to make concessions to the central government, what do you think were the primary reasons? Select three from the following list and rank them in order of importance.

Generally, the views and concerns of your prefecture and the municipalities in it are different, but when your prefecture has been persuaded by the municipalities to do something, what do you think were the main reasons? From the following list, select the three you think were most effective and rank them in order of importance.

[a]The figures in parentheses are the total number of "no answer" responses in each category.

and the third was the support of politicians. Compared with the municipalities, no one response stands out particularly for persuasion by the national government. Since cases of persuasion by the national government are not rare, I suspect that the responses I provided were inadequate, which is why the answer "other" was frequently chosen. It appears that the reasons for persuasion by the national government are varied. When I picked out examples from the "other" category, I was able to divide them as follows: (1) the issue is still unresolved, and therefore there is no agreement; (2) compliance is inevitable when the power of the state is invoked (for example, with the enactment of laws); and (3) we go along because the situation is beyond our control.

PREFECTURAL SIZE

After the war, the position of the prefectures was threatened by the status of the governors and by the question of their size. The size issue—as seen in the proposals for a regional *(dōshū)* system (from the Fourth Advisory Council on the Local Government System) or a local government agency (from the First Provisional Administrative Reform Commission)—immediately became a question of authority, but size per se could also become a major political issue. In a 1981 meeting of a committee of the Second Provisional Administrative Reform

Table 13 *Size of Prefecture*

Type of Prefecture	Area (%)			N
	Too Large	*Just Right*	*Too Small*	
Rural	27	60	13	15
Quasi-urban	6	77	18	17
Urban	9	55	36	11
Total	14	65	21	43

QUESTION: As far as administration is concerned, what do you think of the present size of your prefecture?

Commission (Daini Rinchō), the issue of enlarging the prefectures ultimately faded, but the inefficiently small size of the prefectures was clearly an issue. And even though the *dōshū* system and the consolidation of Osaka, Nara, and Wakayama prefectures, which the business world has advocated since the mid-1960s, acknowledge the status of publicly elected governors, they too make size an issue.

Table 13 analyzes the responses, broken down into the three categories of urbanism, to a question about size. Overall, 65 percent of the governors said that the present size of their prefecture was just right, 14 percent said it was too large, and 21 percent said it was too small. A number of governors of urban areas said "too small," and many governors of rural areas said "too large," as one might expect. But on further consideration, perhaps the nine (21 percent) who said "too small" are too few. If a presently serving governor responds "too small," he may fear creating new political problems in his relations with the surrounding prefectures, so that a response of "just right" may reflect a political decision. In looking at individual interviews, we discovered a few cases where, in prefectures where most government leaders said "too small," the governors actually said "just right." If they did not take political considerations into account, we would expect the number of governors who said "too small" to be slightly larger.

Table 4 suggested that the governors would like more authority in their relations with the national government. In order to find out why they wanted more authority, we asked them what they thought the most important prefectural functions were (table 14). These functions imply the governors' understanding of the essential character of the prefectures. The response categories were drawn from the categories of local

Table 14 *Principal Functions*

	Wide-Area (%)	Standardi-zation (%)	Liaison and Coordi-nation (%)	Supple-mentary (%)	No Answer (%)	N
First answer	74	16	5	0	5	15
Second answer	7	42	19	28	5	17
Third answer	9	14	54	19	5	11
Fourth answer	5	23	19	49	5	43

government activities specified in Article 2, Section 6, of the Local Government Act. For the number 1, or most important, category, the great majority of the governors selected operations covering a wide area. Wide-area operations refer to transmunicipal functions that the prefectures carry out independently of the national government or the municipalities; these include such public activities as the development and conservation of water resources or the development of the local economy. Next in importance were standardization functions, which ensure the consistency of administration through the imposition of national or prefectural standards on the municipalities. These include most of the regulatory functions that are delegated by the central government. Third was the function of fostering communication between the national government and the municipalities and coordinating the interests of the municipalities. Last was the function of supplementing the needs of the municipalities in cases where they cannot do their job because of their small size or financial burdens. None of the governors ranked this first.

Because of limitations of space, I cannot present all the data, but a breakdown according to the rural-urban scale (table 15) reveals the following: all the groups chose wide-area functions as most important, but the urban governors were most likely to choose this response. Although the table does not cover this, if we differentiate second-ranked functions according to the rural-urban scale, rural governors choose standardization functions, and urban governors chose liaison and coordination ones. In general, rural prefectures showed a stronger tendency to regard the functions of the national government as important, reflecting either their socioeconomic conditions or their subordinate culture, with its relative submissiveness to the "orders."

From the length of the debates in the Second Rinchō, we can see that size is an ongoing problem, requiring political sensitivity. We can also

Table 15 *Most Important Prefectural Functions (Governors' First Choice)*

Type of Prefecture	Wide-Area (%)	Standardi-zation (%)	Liaison and Coordi-nation (%)	Supplemen-tary (%)	No Answer (%)	N
Rural	67	20	13	0	0	15
Quasi-urban	71	24	0	0	6	17
Urban	91	0	0	0	9	11
Average	74	16	5	0	5	

grasp the governors' rejection of plans for broad administrative areas from a Kyōdō News Service (Kyōdō Tsūshinsha) survey of local leaders following the Second Rinchō's first report. Table 16 shows the position of governors regarding the *dōshū* system in comparison with the positions of mayors. According to this survey, local government leaders as a whole disliked the system. Some of the mayors approved, but only a small percentage. The governors were unanimously opposed. Two reasons were given for this opposition. The governors in particular said "because it violates decentralization" (although a greater absolute number of the governors said "because there is no need for reform"). As we saw in table 13, nine (21 percent) of the governors felt that the small size of their prefecture was an issue; but the Kyōdō News Service data suggest that this group would also be opposed to a system of fewer, larger regions. The responses indicate that size is definitely a political issue. If we ask the opinion of governors about a reform that will decrease their numbers and shake up the prefectural system, it is unsurprising that they express opposition. Therefore, in spite of the unanimous opposition to the *dōshū* system, we must stress that fifteen governors said that prefectural size was a problem (a total of those who said "too large" or "too small").

One more thing: as we see from the emphasis on "decentralization" in table 6, the governors saw present-day central-local relations as problematic because of the authority system. The governors hoped to expand their functions by enhancing their authority, as the data from the Kyōdō News Service survey in table 17 show. This survey asked, in connection with the Second Rinchō, what was most important in the allocation of administrative projects. The governors stressed that programs should devolve onto the local governments. For mayors, too, this re-

Table 16 *Dōshū System*

Official	Opinion about the System (%)					
	Should be Introduced	*No Need for Reform*	*Violates Decentralization*	*Not Interested*	*Other*	*N*
Governor	0	55	34	0	11	47
City mayor	18	58	14	5	5	595
Town or village mayor	14	68	10	6	2	2,169

QUESTION: What do you think of the dōshū system as a form of wide-area local administration? Choose one response.
SOURCE: Kyōdō News Service 1982.

sponse was the first choice, but they were also relatively concerned about the issue of financial burdens. Even in the present pattern of distribution of functions (*jimu*), they demanded either that the burden be completely the responsibility of higher government levels or that the necessary financial resources be provided. So far I have used the term *functions* to refer to the businesses of government. Functions are not the same thing as authority; they may be simply "duties" or "jobs." Therefore, it is not clear from the mere distribution of "functions" what degree of legal authority or political power is being distributed. But in cases where programs are distributed to local governments, even in cases where supervisory authority is reserved for the national government, it is clear that, to some degree, essential authority is given to the local governments. Therefore, according to table 17, the redistribution of programs (or powers in this context) was overwhelmingly (98 percent) chosen by the governors. In sum, with regard to the administrative reform of central-local relations, the governors saw authority, and the mayors saw finance, as the central issue.

This analysis of the results of the gubernatorial interview survey can be summarized as follows.

First, with regard to the causes of confrontation, "uniformity of national policies" was the reason most stressed by the governors for conflict in their relations with the national government. Although such uniformity does have the virtue of ensuring administrative equity and stability, it also tends toward inflexibility. This quality permeates Japan's central-local relations. On the other hand, the role of politicians was great in the persuasion of the national government. This information

Table 17 *Distribution of Administrative Functions*

Official	Most Important Criterion of Distribution (%)			
	A	*B*	*C*	*N*
Governor	98	0	2	47
City mayor	62	7	30	595
Town or village mayor	57	12	30	2,169

QUESTION: What do you think is most important in the distribution of administrative functions? (A) Programs of immediate concern to the residents should be allocated to local government. (B) Standardized national programs should be increased so that administrative services are equitable across regions. (C) The present distribution is good, but responsibility for tasks should correspond to responsibility for costs.
SOURCE: Kyōdō News Service 1982.

suggests that, as I note elsewhere, the political route is a powerful one in central-local relations. This is an important component of the horizontal political competition model. As the cause of their confrontations with the municipalities, the governors underlined different interests. Such differences are inevitable. When we look at the data regarding the success of persuasion, the response of the majority was "appropriateness of the policy involved." This is a textbook answer, but we can clearly see in it the ideology that the governors wished to emphasize. There was also a realistic acknowledgment of municipal dependence on the prefectures in, for example, financial matters. Frank responses were given about instances of being persuaded by the municipalities, but clear answers were not obtained about the national government because the responses provided were inadequate. The leading reason for successful persuasion by the municipalities was "appropriateness of the policy." In persuasion of the low by the high, it is notable that the intervention of politicians was very rare.

As regards size, fifteen governors, or 35 percent, felt that the size of their prefecture was an issue, but in the opinions elicited by Kyōdō News Service, everyone responded negatively about the *dōshū* system. In effect, these responses were a defense of the status quo. Generally, there was a defense of the status quo in regard to other issues of administrative reform as well, but the gubernatorial views were supportive of moves in the direction of decentralization.

Essentially, then, gubernatorial inclinations in relation to the national government are always to defend the status quo, constantly make demands, and if the chance arises, aim at decentralization. Compared with

Table 18 *Authority and Confrontation: A Summary of Variables*

Variable	Urban Prefectures	Semi-urban Prefectures	Rural Prefectures
Authority vis-à-vis center	Too little	Just right	Just right
Authority vis-à-vis municipalities	Too little	Too great	Too little
Confrontation with center	Tending toward "frequent"	Tending toward "infrequent"	Tending toward "frequent"
Confrontation with municipalities	Tending toward "infrequent"	Tending toward "infrequent"	Tending toward "infrequent"

the realism of the mayors, with their concern for financial problems, the governors are more ideological. This seems to indicate that governors are strongly conscious of their roles as representatives of their regions. As table 3 showed, 98 percent of the governors saw themselves as representatives of their regions. They feel it is gradually becoming more difficult to change the present situation in regard to the size and authority of intermediate bodies. But because the prefectures are intermediate bodies, they cannot help becoming caught in a tug of war.

This analysis just presented can be summarized as shown in table 18. As the data regarding conflict and authority revealed, the governors are intermediaries between a strong central government and weak municipalities. Urban governors in seeking greater power from the national government (their authority was "too little"), evinced a positive attitude as agents of their region (conflict was "frequent"). Rural governors were more comfortable with the framework of the present power structure (their authority was "just right"), but they too display an activist attitude, that is, their confrontations with the national government were also frequent. They too were strongly inclined to push local interests upon the central government. The governors of quasi-urban areas were most affirmative of the present situation. The three categories can be arranged as follows.

Urban governors are dissatisfied with the authority structure laid out by the national government, in their relations with both the municipalities and the national government. Therefore, to the extent that they try to act positively, they cannot avoid conflict with either the national government or the municipalities.

Quasi-urban governors' dissatisfaction with the authority structure is minor, in relation both to the national government and to the municipalities—they even replied that their authority was too great in relation to the municipalities. Therefore, since they are trying to work within the existing framework, confrontation with either the national government or the municipalities rarely arises.

Rural governors, too, are activists. They have considerable conflict with the national government, but *within* the framework of the authority structure created by the national government. Because they are activists, they are dissatisfied with their authority in relation to the municipalities but, given the passivity of the municipalities, there are few disagreements.

In sum, the governors of urban and rural areas are activists, and the governors of quasi-urban areas support the status quo. I will discuss the two types of activism in detail below, but here I should touch on how we should regard the quasi-urban support for the status quo. One interpretation sees it as a result of regional changes that have occurred in both cities and rural areas during the past twenty years. That is, in contrast to areas of overpopulation and depopulation, whose local governments were forced to respond actively, areas in between experienced little intensification of their problems, so that a more relaxed stance by their governors sufficed. Second, because the standards for national policies and operations were created using in-between areas rather than cities or rural areas as the yardstick, it seems plausible that the local governments of these regions would easily feel satisfied.

Rural Activism and Urban Activism

Governors are in lively contact with the political actors of the central government, both as agents of the municipalities and for the sake of their own prefectural administrations. Local finances depend to a high degree on the central government, and many national policies are adopted for local purposes. Therefore, for both prefectures and municipalities, the central government must be the object of incessant lobbying.

Masumi Junnosuke (1969: 12) once suggested, based on his observation of the early postwar period, that the political significance of the elec-

Table 19 *Frequency of Contact with Minister of Home Affairs*
         and Various Ministries

Type of Prefecture	Minister of Home Affairs	Ministry of Home Affairs	Ministry of Finance	Ministry of Health and Welfare	Ministry of Agriculture, Forestry, and Fisheries	Ministry of Construction	Ministry of Transportation
Rural	87	100	87	74	93	93	93
Quasi-urban	76	100	83	71	94	100	82
Urban	100	100	82	73	46	73	73

NOTE: Respondents were asked whether they had contact with the Minister of Home Affairs and various other ministries "once every 2–3 days," "once a week," "once a month," "several times a year," and "less than once a year." The table shows the percentage who replied "several times a year" or more.

tion of governors is that local lobbying activities, which were contained at the prefectural level during the prewar period, have expanded and extended all the way to the center. Certainly, the collision of the enormous political energy of the localities with national politics has become one of the major characteristics of postwar Japanese politics. Many have criticized this as a part of the politics of naked self-interest, but it is undeniably one aspect of the democratic process. As studies of Japanese political history make clear (see Mikuriya 1986, for example), such politics arose in the prewar period, but the postwar scale became possible only through the framework of the new Japanese constitution. The following section interprets data concerning the actions of the governors—the center of this lobbying process—directed at the state.

According to table 19, rural governors tend to have more contact than urban governors with line ministries, such as Transportation, Construction, and Agriculture, Forestry, and Fisheries. Urban governors are also in active contact with the central ministries, but markedly less so than are rural governors, except with regard to the Ministries of Home Affairs and Finance. The common point of Home Affairs and Finance is that, unlike line ministries, they do not share specific activities, such as road construction or education, with the prefectures and that they are responsible for negotiating with local governments about implementing fiscal resources. In effect, from these simple data we derive the impression that the urban governors' reliance on the center is related to financial resource issues and that they try to stay independent of guidance from the other ministries.

Most of a governor's contact with the center is connected to the compilation of the budget. Therefore, differences between urban and rural governors can also be clearly seen in the strategies they use to acquire their budgets (table 20). Because the drawing up of the budget is under the powerful control of the ruling party, winning benefits from the national budget necessitates an approach to the ruling party. Accordingly, the question becomes: From whom within the ruling party should one seek assistance, and how often? Among the governors we surveyed, 80 percent of the rural governors responded that they approached their locally elected LDP Diet members, while urban governors were divided evenly between the LDP leadership and local Diet members (see table 21).

Three interpretations are possible. First, as the people with political responsibility for the regions at the heart of the country's social and economic activity, urban governors generally have more prestige than rural governors; therefore, they can meet directly with the leading echelon of the LDP. The same tendency exists in France (Sidney Tarrow, personal communication 1977). It is thus easier for urban governors to avoid excessive dependence on locally elected Diet members and to maintain their autonomy.

Second, we can explain governors' actions to a considerable extent by the electoral system. Under the Japanese electoral system in rural regions, many prefectures had only one small voting district with only two or three seats, and most of the winners were members of the LDP. In urban regions, prefectures had multiple districts—in the case of Tokyo, there were eleven—and each district elected three or four or even eight Diet members. But the number of LDP seats in urban areas, on the average, was only one in five. For this reason, it was easy in rural areas to form a cooperative relationship between the governors and the locally elected LDP Diet members. The governors assisted conservative politicians in getting benefits for the local area, and the conservative Diet members helped the governors get special subsidies and other benefits from the central ministries. But because the governors of urban areas had pluralistic political bases, they could not afford to seek aid exclusively from Diet members of any party. More important, power in the prefectural assemblies was not concentrated in one party. Leftist opposition party politicians were for long weak at the center, and conservatives were weak in the urban areas. Even though the LDP was the ruling party at the center, exclusive cooperation with LDP Diet members could endanger the political position of

Table 20 *Efforts to Influence the National Budget*

Type of Prefecture	A	B	C	D	E	*N*
Rural	7	73	87	73	93	15
Quasi-urban	24	65	88	94	94	17
Urban	27	82	91	82	91	11

NOTE: Respondents were asked to rank five stages of the budgetary process for the degree of effort they exerted. The table shows the percentage who replied "extreme effort" or "considerable effort" for each stage. (A) When the prime minister determines basic policies. (B) When the ministries and bureaus determine the following year's programs. (C) When the ministries and bureaus estimate the following year's budgetary needs. (D) When the Ministry of Finance drafts a budget. (E) When the government as a whole drafts its budget.

Table 21 *Liberal Democratic Party (Jimintō) Posts Approached in order to Influence the National Budget*

	Rural Prefecture (%)	Semiurban Prefecture (%)	Urban Prefecture (%)	All (%)
Party president, heads of factions, three top party officials	20	29	46	30
Policy Affairs Research Council (PARC) committees	0	0	0	0
PARC plenary session	0	0	0	0
Executive council	0	0	0	0
Members of relevant Diet committees	0	0	0	0
Locally elected Diet members	80	71	46	67
Individual Diet members	0	0	0	0
Other	0	0	9	2
No contact	0	0	0	0
N	15	17	11	43

the governor because of his relationship with his own prefectural assembly.

Third and most important, rural prefectures—including their governors—have been deeply entangled in a kind of reciprocal political process (cf. Gouldner 1964). On the one hand, local governments rely on the central ministries and agencies for money, technical assistance in policy making, and legal advice. On the other hand, the central ministries and agencies—using the national political process and particularly the political processes relating to interest groups and the compilation of the budget—rely on local governments to pressure the political parties to advance their own ministerial interests; they especially rely on local governments to implement various ministerial projects. During the period when the budget is being drafted, lobbying organizations flock around the LDP and the Finance Ministry, but many lobbying groups are directed by coalitions of local representatives that include publicly elected leaders and interest groups. For example, the Sewage Association has deep ties to the Urban Bureau of the Construction Ministry and the special LDP committee on sewage measures. The Parks and Green Belts Association is closely linked to one bureau in the Construction Ministry and the special LDP committee on parks and green belts. The Japan Harbors Association is closely linked to the Bureau of Harbors in the Transportation Ministry and the transportation committee of the LDP Policy Affairs Research Council. In negotiations with their LDP Diet members, the regional representatives stand in the forefront and the interest groups remain in the background (Hirose 1981: 164–65). With this pressure in the background, the Diet members exercise leadership in determining party policy and bring their influence to bear on the national government.

Let us describe several features of this process, using agricultural policy as an example (Hirose 1981: 94–97, 144–49). Despite the powerful pressure of agricultural groups, in the budget for 1978 the LDP decided not to raise the producer price of rice (a subsidy to growers). Because of accumulated government deficits, the leaders of the LDP were driven to reform the budget fundamentally. But a general election was looming ahead. Consequently, Finance Minister Watanabe and the secretary general of the LDP agreed to appropriate 20 billion yen (40 million dollars in 1981) for the Program for Promoting Emergency Measures in Agricultural, Forestry, and Fishing Villages (Nōringyogyō Sonraku Shinkō Kinkyū Taisaku Jigyō). The plan was intended to foster regional solidarity by constructing facilities for improving health, advancing welfare, and encouraging exchanges among citizens. The result of this vague definition of purpose was that the municipalities were given broad discretionary powers. Six hundred twenty municipalities qualified to receive subsidies. In the execution of the project, the prefectures first received shares of the subsidy, gen-

erally in proportion to the number of eligible municipalities they contained; they then allocated their portion of the subsidy to the municipalities under their jurisdiction. Here the prefectures had a good deal
of discretion. The municipalities first stressed their own qualifications
on the national level; then they fought a second round in the competition for subsidies at the prefectural level. At the national level, LDP
Diet groups known as *zoku* were influential, brokering the interests of
the pressure groups with the people who set the policies. In the Program for Promoting Emergency Measures, one of the two agriculture-
related *zoku* was important, and the prefectures that dispatched influential local figures to the central *zoku* received a greater share of the
subsidy. In this case, Yamagata prefecture, protected by Kondō Tet-
suo, an influential member of the agricultural *zoku*, received advanta-
geous treatment.

The next year as well, rice prices were left untouched. The Program
for Promoting Emergency Measures, established the previous year, was
abolished by the Finance Ministry because of the need to curtail expenses, but the leaders of the LDP, in order to compensate for the loss,
introduced a new policy, with virtually the same objective. Called the
Agricultural Structural Reform Village Subsidy Program (Nōgyō Kōzō
Kaizen Sonraku Hojo Jigyō), it used the same methods as the year before to appropriate virtually the same budgetary amount. Nevertheless,
one can see important differences in the implementation of the two policies. Allocations under the Program for Promoting Emergency Measures were made in an extremely political manner, whereas under the
Agricultural Reform Program, the allocations were made in Tokyo on
the basis of objective bureaucratic standards. While the politics of forming a new cabinet after the election was still under way, the bureaucracy
nearly completed its budget for local allotments. This kind of decision
belongs to the sphere of political-administrative bargaining. An implicit
rule of bargaining is applied in such a way that unless the parties offer an
opinion, bureaucratic decisions and methods will naturally proceed on a
routine schedule. Japanese policy making follows the "administrative
style" (Muramatsu 1981b: chap. 5). Because the balance of power at the
center tilts at times toward the bureaucracy and at times toward the political parties, local governments must continually be careful in determining their strategy vis-à-vis the center.

Japanese central-local relations seem especially to involve LDP Diet
members and rural governors. For example, LDP Diet members from
rural areas are always requested to attend the national conferences of

agricultural organizations. During the national rice conference held in 1979 in Tokyo, 319 of 763 Diet members (including proxies) attended (Tachibana 1980: 336–37). The agricultural committee of the LDP Policy Affairs Research Council held a meeting and, based on the decisions made there, was able to influence the government's Rice Price Advisory Council—which meets to collect the opinions of experts in setting the next year's rice price.

The urban governors, who rule politically important regions, have a variety of political resources, which include cooperation with the various political parties. In particular, specialized techniques and information are their most important resources. The bureaucratic structures of the urban prefectures even have the power to challenge the national bureaucracy. According to some appraisals, the expertise for regulating pollution at the disposal of the bureaucratic organs of metropolitan Tokyo or the city of Yokohama is superior to that of the state bureaucracy. Many governors are themselves able politicians. For these reasons, urban governors can be independent of both locally elected Diet members and the central bureaucratic structure. Nevertheless, in spite of indications that they want autonomy, urban governors from early on have been—paradoxically—more active and more vigorous than quasi-urban or rural governors in their pressure on the budgetary process (table 20). Compared with quasi-urban and rural governors, urban governors are more likely to work directly with the LDP president and the three top party executives (secretary general, chair of the executive council, and chair of the Policy Affairs Research Council). A breakdown of the careers of the eleven urban governors in this chapter shows that four had been bureaucrats in the central ministries and agencies (including the governor of Kyoto, who was briefly a member of the Diet after retiring from the bureaucracy), three were local bureaucrats, two were leftist politicians, and two had been businessmen. Such careers do not explain the governors' contact with the three party executives. Rather, it is because they occupy the office of governor in urban areas that they have sufficient influence to negotiate directly with top LDP officers.

As I described above, there is a complicated explanation for why governors of urban areas rely relatively little on locally elected LDP Diet members. To supplement this explanation, let me say that the plans that urban governors bring to their negotiations with the center are, for financial and other reasons, too much for a single locally elected Diet member. At the same time, it is possible that, in fact, the governors and the LDP have a similar dependence on the farming villages, but since other parties are also strong within their prefecture, they are hesitant to make gestures of reliance on the LDP alone.

Because they expect relatively little of the central ministries and agencies and of locally elected Diet members, and because there are legislative considerations that limit their reliance on the LDP, urban governors vigorously cultivate independent political bases of support. It may be for this reason that prefectures in urban areas have recently begun to intervene in policy domains in competition with the municipalities. According to the analysis of Takagi Shōsaku (1979: 15–17), the prefectures compete with the municipalities in at least three ways. First, they participate directly in programs already undertaken by the municipalities (for example, in water supply). Second, implementation of new prefectural functions (for example, assistance for the hospitalization of children) is mandated to the municipalities. Third, there are cases where the prefectures provide financial incentives to municipalities in order to promote existing municipal policies (for example, the building of city libraries). "Community development projects" have been adopted by many urbanized prefectures, but they probably fall into the first category. These projects respond to the need to rebuild urban neighborhoods where social relations have become cold and fragmented. Saitama prefecture is said to be particularly enthusiastic about community projects, but its efforts are related to the fact that Saitama is a rapidly urbanizing area in the Tokyo region. In the case of Okayama prefecture, community development projects have been related to the broad delegation of powers that comes with newly established local facilities of central agencies. But it is debatable whether it is desirable for the prefectures to intervene in the policy domains with which the municipalities should be concerned.

The view presented in this chapter can be related to concrete investigations leading toward the classification of interactions between the prefectures and the central government. Noteworthy in this literature is Nakano Minoru's 1986 empirical study of prefecture A. While noting that (compared with Tokyo) the autonomy of prefecture A is rather weak, Nakano skillfully analyzes the increase of political influence in this prefecture. He divides the central budget for the prefecture resolved as follows: (1) budget items for which distribution is carried out smoothly at the initiative of the center within the framework that the center has created, (2) budget items for which the local government has pressured the center by mobilizing politicians or former bureaucrats, and (3) budget subsidies acquired through the individual lobbying of powerful politicians. In all these cases, closely coordinated interaction takes place among Diet members, prefectural assembly members, and prefectural officials, and the typology of these interactions is variously discussed. In general, it is suggested that the scope of the activity of Diet members is broad and the role of the governors is expanding. Nakano's study seems to suggest the same direction as the results of the gubernatorial study presented in this chapter.

CHAPTER 4

The Municipalities

*The Implementation of National Policies
and Financial Subsidies*

The Implementation of National Policies

DIMENSIONS OF A NEW THEORY

In the first three chapters I have made the following points. First, in addition to the administrative factors that earlier theories have stressed, political factors are important in any consideration of Japan's central-local relations. Moreover, there is political competition both within and between local governments. Chapter 3 gave an account only of competition between local governments; competition within government was not discussed, but I think it is self-evident. Moreover, our analysis has focused primarily on the prefectures (governors), but the same model can be applied to the municipalities. In this chapter I hope to demonstrate its applicability by analyzing the implementation of several central government projects at the local level.

Next, in analyzing specific cases, we should be conscious of the division of labor between the municipalities, prefectures, and central government in the central-local system of shared operations. Theories of Japanese local government often generalize legalistically about "ordinary local public bodies" without consciously distinguishing between the prefectures and the municipalities, although there is a great difference between the political roles of the two. In chapter 3 I argued that the prefectures are not the partners of the central ministries and agencies, as is commonly believed. The prefectures have been "localized" by the popular election of governors. In this chapter, however, while analyzing the activities of the municipalities in the implementation of central policies, I will indicate the role of the prefectures as regulators of the municipalities. The prefectures are therefore intermediate bodies. By contrast, because the municipalities are local governments in direct contact with the citizens, an analysis of them rather than the prefectures can generate a far more nuanced view of local political life.

In the course of operations that involve the center and local governments, the prefectures mediate between central plans and local needs. Their role is like the fulcrum of a seesaw: sometimes they reflect the plans of the center and forcefully lead the municipalities, while at others they consider the feelings of the municipalities and restrain the plans of the center. In analyzing these actions, we will demonstrate the effectiveness of the models of horizontal political competition and overlapping authority, and at the same time enrich their content.

The hypothesis underlying this chapter is that the horizontal competition model can be applied to municipalities as well as to prefectures. Because municipalities also possess political will, they too engage in lobbying the central ministries and political parties. In the second section of this chapter, I address this fact using survey data from municipal leaders about national subsidies. In the case studies presented in the first section, I consider how the ideas and plans of the central government are opposed or harmonized with the will of the municipalities during the implementation process. Central and local governments occupy a relationship of overlapping authority, sharing operations in everything they do, but our interest lies in the specifics of that interdependence and how conflict within it is resolved. Because my approach focuses on the bargaining processes of the actors involved, I stress the differences between specific projects and specific people. But the bargaining itself takes place under the following general conditions.

First, central-local bargaining is not a onetime event. It lasts for a relatively long time—often much longer than the term of office of a local executive—and is a reciprocal relationship. Second, the center and the local governments are not equals. The state is sovereign, and even though the constitution affirms the principle of local autonomy, the role of local government can be reduced when necessary. The authority of the central government is clear. It can choose one of two alternatives in cases where the localities sabotage or fail to implement the delegated functions: they may secure compliance through the courts (*mandamus* proceeding), or they may directly implement policy to the exclusion of the wishes of localities or even dismiss insubordinate mayors or governors. The ministerial bureaucratic system is usually cited as the executor of central authority, but I would like to point out that Diet members and political parties are also agents and targets of the authority of the central government. Therefore, the usual opposition of Diet members to reductions in individual subsidies, which is problematic from the point of view of local government theory, is not surprising. At the same time that national politicians are agents of local interests directed toward the center, on another level it is to their advantage to maintain state authority.

The third point is related to the proposition that "policy determines politics." One may argue that some issues never become part of the intergovernmental political process. For example, in his critique of my argument that there is a great potential for local government in Japan, Mizuguchi Norihito (1984) asserts that local government is structurally limited and that because of these limitations there are some things that cannot become issues in central-local relations. But I think that in actual local politics anything can become an issue. And this fact is a major characteristic of local politics in postwar Japan. For example, international relations and national defense problems are usually considered to be the exclusive jurisdiction of the state. But the issue of U.S. army tanks passing through city streets made the legitimacy of the U.S.-Japan Security Treaty as a whole a municipal issue in the city of Sagamihara. Recently, it also became a matter of political debate in the city of Zushi whether the site (on a U.S. military base) of the former Ikego ammunition depot was an urban park or a foreign policy issue. And ours is an era when local governments cannot help but think of national financial and manufacturing policies as their own problems as well. Still, some issues clearly become the object of central-local bargaining more easily than others.

At this point, I would like to proceed to look at the central-local relationship of overlapping authority at the municipal level.

FOUR POLICIES
OF THE CENTRAL GOVERNMENT

First, let me explain the methodology of the following case studies. The focus of the analysis is the findings of a joint project carried out in 1984 by Ōmori Wataru, Nakamura Akira, Takeshita Yuzuru, Hashimoto Nobuyuki, Kitahara Tetsuya, and myself (Muramatsu Michio, chair, "A Study of the Modes of Participation and Responsibility in the Policy Implementation Process," Gyōsei Kanri

Kenkyū Sentā [Center for the Study of Administrative Management] 1985). We selected four policies established by the central government: the introduction of a system of partial patient payment that accompanied a revision of the senior citizens health law, nursery schools, public housing, and the conversion of agricultural land. Of the first three, two were under the jurisdiction of the Ministry of Health and Welfare and one under the Ministry of Construction, but all should be considered welfare programs. Since Japan, like other advanced industrial nations, is gradually becoming a welfare state, it was relevant to investigate such projects in order to get at the characteristics of modern Japanese administration and central-local relations. The conversion of agricultural land is qualitatively different from the other three, and it allows us to check on whether we can generalize from them.

We chose six cities for our study—two with leftist administrations, two with conservative leadership, and two that were evenly divided between progressives and conservatives. ("Evenly divided" is an admittedly imprecise category. We chose city A, in which a conservative mayor had just succeeded a long-serving progressive mayor, and city C, in which the mayor received support from both the progressives and the conservatives.) Among them, three were in the metropolitan Tokyo area, two were suburban cities in the Osaka area, and one was in Ehime prefecture and not near a large city; all were cities of moderate importance (table 22).

As already discussed, when programs involve both the center and local governments, the prefectures mediate between the goals of the center and the needs of the local areas. Their role is either to reflect the plans of the center and lead the municipalities or to reflect the opinions of the municipalities and curb the center.

Let us now, for each of the four programs, consider the plans of the center, the intermediary function of the prefectures, and the actual implementation by the municipalities.

Public Housing. Local government public housing projects for lower-income groups are based on the Public Housing Law of 1951. Under this law, the projects depend on national-local cooperation; their goal is "to build housing that is sufficient for a wholesome, decent life and, by leasing these residences to low-income people at low rents, to help stabilize the livelihood of the people and promote social welfare." Public housing is divided into two categories according to the income of the residents: the national government subsidizes half the construction expenses paid by the local government for higher-income housing and

Table 22 *Characteristics of Cities Studied*

	City A	City B	City C	City D	City E	City F
Location	Near Tokyo	Near Tokyo	Near Tokyo	Kinki (Osaka-Kyoto) area	Kinki (Osaka-Kobe) area	Not near a major city
Population	100,000 (large youthful population)	160,000 (small youthful population)	270,000 (large youthful population)	70,000 (large youthful population)	175,000 (large youthful population)	130,000 (small youthful, large elderly population)
Mayor's political base	Conservative[a]	Progressive[b]	Middle-of-the-road[c]	Conservative[d]	Conservative[e]	Progressive[f]
Political composition of city council	LDP: 2 Socialist: 4 Democratic Socialist: 2 Kōmeitō: 4 Communist: 3 Independents: 17 (Total: 32)	LDP: 1 Socialist: 2 Democratic Socialist: 1 Kōmeitō: 5 Communist: 6 New Liberal: 2 Independents: 23 (Total: 40)	LDP: 1 Socialist: 5 Democratic Socialist: 2 Kōmeitō: 5 Communist: 5 Independents: 11 (Total: 29)	LDP: 12 Socialist: 3 Kōmeitō: 3 Communist: 6 Minor party: 1 (Total: 25)	LDP: 2 Socialist: 2 Democratic Socialist: 1 Kōmeitō: 4 Communist: 4 Independents (conservative): 16 Independents (progressive): 1 (Total: 30)	Socialist: 6 Kōmeitō: 4 Communist: 3 Independents: 23 (Total: 36)

[a] For the preceding fourteen years, the mayor was affiliated with the progressive wing, with Socialist and Communist support. The present mayor was nominated by the LDP.

[b] Nominated by the Socialists, Communists, Social Democrats, and progressives.

[c] Nominated by the Kōmeitō, New Liberal, and Social Democratic parties, with the support of the Socialists and Democratic Socialists.

[d] Nominated by the LDP, Socialist, Kōmeitō, Democratic Socialist, New Liberal, and Social Democratic parties.

[e] Nominated by the LDP, Democratic Socialist, and New Liberal parties, with the support of the Kōmeitō.

[f] Nominated by the Socialist Party.

two-thirds of the construction expenses for lower-income housing, in order to encourage the involvement of local governments in this program. Thus, the implementation of public housing programs is related to the initiatives of local governments. At the same time, however, their construction—which is part of the Five-Year Housing Construction Plan, based in turn on the Housing Construction Planning Law—is part of an overall national policy that addresses the housing situation nationwide. Consequently, there is sometimes a discrepancy between local tendencies to use the program to provide public housing to low-income people and the national policy to meet the general demand for housing throughout the country, depending on the economy at a given time. According to Nakamura Akira's analysis of municipal public housing projects (Gyōsei Kanri Kenkyū Sentā 1985: 65–66), during the period of rapid economic growth the Ministry of Construction made public housing part of its Five-Year Housing Construction Plan, and it used this program to respond to rapid urbanization. Between 1945 and 1955 the plans of the central government, which inclined toward social welfare, moved in the direction of large-scale construction. In this period, according to Nakamura, the central government (in this case, the Ministry of Construction) operated in top-down style: it made its allocations to the prefectures and through them to the municipalities.

This was also a period during which the municipalities were crying out for an increase in public housing. They competed for the limited subsidies from the center, and the prefectures exercised a good deal of discretion in their relations with the municipalities. It was reported, for example, that in prefecture Z (ruled by a conservative governor), there had been discrimination in the treatment of leftist-run city F relative to the other municipalities (Gyōsei Kanri Kenkyū Sentā 1985: 65–66). But in the municipalities in urban prefectures the desire for the construction of public housing declined beginning in the 1970s, and there were signs of declining efficiency in the implementation of the program. Then the central government began to pressure the prefectures for the construction of public housing in order to use up the budget. And many prefectures, accepting the will of the central government, worked to persuade the municipalities. The fact that the conservative government of prefecture Z later came to favor housing projects pursued in leftist city F seems related to this change in attitude. Since 1981, the total budget has been rigorously controlled through constraints on the budgets of each ministry and agency (Muramatsu 1983b). Under these conditions of financial distress, it will be interesting to see whether the budget for public housing is curtailed. In any case, regardless of its bad reputation at the local level, for the central government to put forward a negative attitude toward public housing would seem to contradict its earlier intent. Therefore, the prefectures complied with the plans of the center and began to work to help in using up the budget.

The activity regarding public housing projects thus grew out of a combination of two factors. On the one hand, there was the dynamics of the national policy process. In the period 1945–55 it took as its primary goal the resolution of the housing shortage. Because it targeted the low-income class, it clearly had a redistributive function, but because it focused on "construction" it fell under the jurisdiction of the Ministry of Construction, not the Ministry of Health and Welfare. (This created some complications in the administration of public housing at the municipal level. One example is the fact that municipalities seek the backing of the welfare office when they recruit tenants for public housing.) A factor that has since constrained the plans of the center, or at least the degree of fulfillment of these plans, is the constrained budget process noted above. Within the Ministry of Construction, in response to the government's zero (or minus) budget ceiling, there is certainly defensive activity by the relevant administrative bodies at the stage where approximate needs are determined. But, once there is a specific budget allocation at the central level, the expenditure of this budget becomes the supreme command of "the system." Relying on its partners at the prefectural level, the Ministry of Construction's Housing Bureau embarks on a strategy to spend the whole allocation.

Another factor is the municipalities. There are changes in the municipal politics of public housing as well, and in the end they determine the number of houses built by the local governments. When we look at the cases in the present study, we discover few requests for the construction of public housing in cities located in metropolitan areas. Difficulties in land acquisition are the official reason, but we can speculate that the cities are disinclined to increase low-income housing because such a policy places them in a disadvantageous situation in terms of both revenue and expenditures. In these cases as well, the cities respond to demands from their own political actors. But public housing does not generate any coherent influence (in votes). Moreover, when the claims of the tenants are isolated from those of their neighborhoods, they have no power because number of voters is small, and when they vote along with the neighborhood associations, the claims of the tenants are completely absorbed by the concerns of the association as a whole. Among the political parties, the Communists and the Kōmeitō give some support to these projects, but not much. Because demand has declined in the metropolitan areas, the budget for public housing is allocated more to other regions. Metropolitan local governments are generally passive about public housing, but insofar as they are in a network of overlapping authority with the related bureaus of the Ministry of Construction and the prefectures, they have to cooperate in expending the budget. For city D, the point of cooperation was "renovation." By showing concern for public housing in the form of renovation, the city showed concern for the low-income classes and also made an effective gesture toward the Communist Party and the Kōmeitō. And the center welcomed the chance to give grants-in-aids for this purpose to city C. In this way, there is mutual dependence between the center and local governments. The municipalities have an opportunity to have their own demands recognized by the prefectures and the center. The center and the prefectures rely on the municipalities for implementation.

　This case shows a central-local overlapping authority game within the framework of a set budget and shrinking operations.

　　　　Partial Payment in Medical Care for the Aged.　Before 1982, under the Geriatric Welfare Law, central government policy was to provide free medical care for people over the age of seventy within a certain income limit. Specifically, when municipal payments under the health insurance and public health insurance laws—which included medical fees for residents over seventy—were not enough to cover all needed medical expenses, the national government made up the difference. The national government bore the responsibility for two-thirds of what was lacking, and the remaining one-third was divided evenly between the prefecture and the municipality. To supplement the national policy (as an independent program), many prefectures and municipalities (1) removed the income limit and devised no-fee policies for all people over seventy and (2) adopted policies broadening the privilege to include residents in their late sixties as well. The national government was tolerant of such practices, respecting the fact that the free medical care policies had originally been initiated by local governments.

　But the expansion of medical payments for the aged and the ineffective use of medical facilities gradually drew criticism, and measures were adopted to counter them. The system of "partial patient payment" was introduced as part of the 1982 Health Law for the Aged. It was a national response to remedy the shortcomings of the previous free treatment policy. According to its provisions, people who received medical treatment through insurance and medical facilities would bear part of the financial burden, paying 400 yen ($1.60) a day as an outpatient or 300 yen ($1.20) a day for hospitalization (which was limited to two months).

This policy change forced the municipalities to consider the following questions: (1) Since the new national policy demanded partial payment by people over seventy, what should they do about the free care for the under-seventy age group that they had independently developed? (2) Should they take steps to compensate people over seventy for the partial burden they now had to bear?

It is clear that the state was motivated by the desire to control fiscal demands. But it was predicted that the municipalities and prefectures would compensate individuals whose financial burden increased under the new system. A Ministry of Health and Welfare administrative guideline therefore said that "compensation by public bodies by means of independent programs runs counter to the spirit of this law and should be strictly restrained." Nevertheless, even in the face of the clearly stated position of the central government, a number of responses were available to the local governments. In one prefecture in the Kansai area, many municipalities adopted independent compensation because, they said, the prefecture agreed with their policy. By contrast, because prefecture X was advising them to follow the policy of "strict restraint" announced by the Ministry of Health and Welfare, city D in our study decided that a program of straight compensation was out of the question and the city itself could only say that it would try something. The details of the responses of the six cities we studied were as follows.

First, in three cases (cities B, C, and E) the prefecture and the city both accepted the national policy and did not establish compensation programs. In one case (city F), officials said that they "were not afraid" of the central government or the prefecture and proceeded to compensate through an independent program. Two cases (cities A and D) took heed of the central policy but exhibited some independence.

Even this simple summary shows that the local governments responded independently, even to a clear policy from the center; in their responses, there were differences corresponding to local conditions. But what were the differences? What kinds of political factors created these differences? In comparison with public housing, which followed the principle of administrative reciprocity, here more political factors regulated local government responses. First, there are clearly differences between progressive and conservative cities. City A, which had been ruled by progressives for fourteen years, strongly stressed the idea of comprehensive welfare, and that seems to have determined the content of its response. In 1984 this city elected a conservative mayor, but he seemed to take on many of the policies of his predecessor. The Socialist Party even refrained from putting up an opposing candidate in order to safely elect the new mayor. In addition, the city council was composed of seventeen conservatives and fifteen leftists, a force able to watch carefully over the course of the previous mayor's policies. Prefecture Z, which includes city A, had a conservative prefectural government that was inclined to act as a mediator for the plans of the center, but it seems to have been unable to influence city A. Similarly, the noted conservative stronghold of prefecture W could not influence city F. In defiance of the national plan, city F established a plan to help pay the fees of the bedridden aged and tried to preserve the equivalent of the previous medical services for the aged lost under the new national policy. According to Kitahara Tetsuya, who studied city F, these measures followed the strong intentions of the mayor; although all parties in the city council were consulted, the council did not play a role in promoting them (Gyōsei Kanri Kenkyū Sentā 1985: 121–22). And in a similarly clear reflection of the mayor's inclinations, city D continued to carry out the will of the center and the prefectures, but established a policy of monetary "consolation gifts" for hospital patients. Unlike city F, however, its motivation seemed to lie in consideration of the local conservative base of political support.

Except for these three cases, our impression is that cities followed the lead of their prefectures in dealing with problems of medical treatment for the aged; it is important therefore to pay attention to prefectural guidance and mediation. In addition, it is possible that the action style of "conservative" mayors is changing. On the one hand they try to follow the plans of the center and the prefecture, but on the other hand they feel a responsibility to their own support base; sometimes they are torn between the two, as shown in the cases we studied. In our survey, half the conservative mayors referred to the center's plan and half to their support base. But in the future, it is likely that conservatives will consider their own local base more than the intentions of the center.

In this instance, where the position of the central government was clear to all, the prefectures in general acted as mediators in compliance with the central government, but they also gave the following reasons for wanting to demonstrate their independence: for leftists, it was the issue of welfare; for conservatives, it was the problem of their support base. In chapter 3 and elsewhere (Muramatsu 1986 [Japanese]), I have argued that rural prefectures tend to become mediators for the center, while urban prefectures tend to become the political coordinators of a variety of local interests. However, although these types of activity are most closely associated with the urban-rural distinction, when one observes prefectures in action, the typology also appears valid for prefectures in general. Specific instances of mediation are apparent in the present case studies. Let us note the differences in the logic of prefectures Y and W, which persuaded cities not to compensate patients. Prefecture W based its decision on the principle of equal standards within the prefecture; prefecture Y placed the intentions of the central government at the forefront. This difference, according to Ōmori and Takeshita (Gyōsei Kanri Kenkyū Sentā 1985: 140–41), can be understood as follows. The government of prefecture W, where the medical association was not very strong, could lead the prefecture by itself, but prefecture Y, where the voice of the local medical association was strong, had to invoke the authority of the central government.

Day Nurseries. The administration of day nurseries is based on the Child Welfare Law of 1947. Municipal operation of day nurseries or preschools has a history dating back to before the war, but here one should note only that prewar day nurseries focused on the children of poor families and that they were inferior to private nursery schools. The day nurseries based on the Child Welfare Law of 1947 also aimed at "children lacking day care," again assuming poor families.

We can infer the central government's plan, first of all from the provisions and spirit of the Child Welfare Law. The state's goal for day care administration, as described in the first section of the law, is first of all the healthy nurturing of children's minds and bodies; therefore, Article 39 calls for administrative measures for children "lacking day care." That is, it provides substitute services for children with no one to take care of them, thereby attempting to promote their welfare. In order to actually implement the administration of day nurseries, facilities must be built and teachers and other necessary personnel deployed. The central government, by making these agency-delegated functions, primarily has the municipalities carry them out. Formerly, in places like metropolitan Osaka, the prefecture ran the day nurseries directly, but under the central plan the prefectures seem to be expected to perform a supervisory function as intermediate bodies. If so, how would the center regard it if the intermediary bodies actively devised their own policies? This point was apparently unforeseen by the central bureaucrats when the Child Welfare Law was put into effect. But the Child Welfare Law itself makes the nation, the prefectures, and the municipalities all responsible and does not exclude active participation by the prefectures. In fact, even though the act of providing the service is entrusted to the municipalities, supplementary prefectural programs are widely carried out in the areas of long-term day care and nurseries for the physically handicapped.

The question is, how much day care service has come to be provided, and in what form? The data on central goals regarding this point are found in the Ministry of Health and Welfare's instructions to local governments and its standards and procedures for making budget allotments. Ministerial instructions were issued in 1955, 1957, and 1961, but only the 1961 instruction is still effective. It concerns entrance standards; specifically, the entrance qualifications include a mother employed at home or outside, households without a mother, a mother giving birth or caring for a sick person, or similar family crises.

The central plan for day nurseries was even vaguer than those for the two previous programs. The entrance standards were transmitted by ministerial instructions as described above, but there was a good deal of discretion possible within the limits of these apparently explicit standards. Therefore, cities established their own standards, based on the general outline. The state's attitude was that any entrance standards within those specified in the instructions were acceptable; financially its general policy was not to complain even if the day nursery rates it specified were not accepted, as long as any resulting costs were covered by independent municipal programs. Its view was the same when services were strengthened by adding more personnel than authorized.

In their mediation, the prefectures generally served as a conduit, without adding any judgment of their own. Besides the routine relaying of procedures, they exercised guidance and oversight to make sure that local entrance standards agreed with national ones. When privately owned and operated day care centers (or what were popularly called "baby hotels") as well as nursery care for handicapped children became public issues, they set up independent supplementary programs. Here, too, they followed in the wake of policies.

As seen in the six cities of this study, municipalities are in general active promoters. Within their financial limits, there is a tendency to set up a large number of independent programs. The extent of the tendency reflects demographic factors such as the number of young housewives, whether that number is increasing or decreasing, and how many private day nurseries exist. But we must also not overlook the political factors, specifically: (1) whether the mayor's own principles and support base are conservative or leftist, (2) the strengths of conservatives and progressives in the city council, and (3) the cohesiveness of citizens' groups. These three factors can be explained as follows. Above all, the more cohesive and demanding the citizens' groups, the more the programs respond to the basic demographic factors described above. In many suburban cities where there are a large number of young housewives and children, the mayors are affiliated with leftists and the city councils are strongly leftist oriented. But even conservative leaders must respond when the demands of the citizens arise from these demographic factors. When we look at the survey results of each city, we see that in city F, because of condition number 3 (low politicization of the citizens), day care issues are left to the judgment of the mayor. Though the mayor of city F personally values other welfare services, his concern for public day care is weak—and so is the administration of city F's day nurseries.

Let us look at the response of city governments when there have been strong demand from the citizens for improvement of day nursery services. Leftist mayors look favorably upon day care administration. Conversely, conservative mayors value at-home nursing; moreover, they lean administratively toward small government, and in social welfare they give more consideration to the aged. In the administration of day care, this conservative or leftist position was a factor of great influence, as shown by the earlier leftist government of city A and by city C in prefecture W during the era of local progressive government, where day care administration was highly emphasized. Conversely, the conservative mayor of city D, whose campaign promise was "Neither retreat nor expansion," expressed an attitude toward day care administration that seemed in the direction of "retreat"; and the policies of the new conservative government of city A weakened the tone of the former administration, which had pursued a "compulsory" or "semicompulsory" day care policy.

I would like to make a few other observations about the links between politics and the administration of day care. First, no matter what the personal opinion of conservative mayors is with regard to the day care, when another political force—specifically, the strong insistence of the citizens—appears, they must respond; while this is a defensive move, in the end it leads to a significant response. Second, the Second Rinchō and the atmosphere of administrative reform it created have generally led to caution about expanding services and, in the area of expenses, to raises in local day care charges as well as the institution of public-private operations or outright privatization. We can discover here as well political factors that influence policy implementation. We do not know from the present study to what extent there are differences between conservatives and progressives in day care fee increases. But from my study of a number of cities in the Kansai area, it appears that conservative mayors are more likely to state clearly that they will do what they must. Cities with leftist mayors, not wanting to stand out from their neighbors, tend to wait for neighboring municipalities to raise fees and then take action themselves a little later. Moreover, the rate of fee increases is slightly smaller in cities run by progressives. This point should be confirmed with better data from further studies. In addition, many cities have established screening committees of specialists to determine standards for admission, and they apply these standards rigorously. In an action characteristic of the Tokyo metropolitan area, the residents tried to realize their own claims by pursuing all available legal procedures. In cities A and C, citizens' groups filed petitions of inquiry, taking the appropriate legal steps to oppose their respective mayors' decisions.

The Conversion of Agricultural Land. Finally, let us consider the conversion of agricultural land. A central plan tried to ensure the rationalization of the conversion with two stages. First, according to the New City Planning Law, boundaries were drawn that divided land into two zones—one in which it was thought that existing farmland should be used to form towns, and one that in principle was not to be urbanized. Next, the conversion of land within the zones not slated for urbanization was strictly regulated, using the Agricultural Land Law and the Agriculture Promotion Law. During both stages, the governors were given ultimate legal authority because it was felt that local governments would find it in their own interests to make the program work. In concrete terms, the state's position regarding conversion was expressed as follows, in a vice-ministerial guideline based on the Agricultural Land Law:

In comparison with the time when the Agricultural Land Law was established, the national economy has developed remarkably, bringing with it changes in the industrial structure, urban population growth, and urban development. In light of this, some conversion of agricultural land cannot be avoided, but in cases where it is planned to build facilities that are not essential to economic development, or to the stability of the people's livelihood, and in cases where we fear that the converted land may not be used and that it will become idle as a result of conversion, we think that we should restrict the conversion of agricultural land with all our might [1959 Permission Standards for Farmland Conversion].

This statement was a warning about conversion of farmland to other purposes, but it recognized the need to respond to the land needs that accompanied economic growth; still, although it cited the example of conversion to golf courses as undesirable, the standards that it provided were unclear. In the drawing of boundaries according to the New City Planning Law and in the approval of conversions, the state seems to have decided that giving authority to the governors would lead to rational decisions, but strong leadership did not emerge in all the prefectures. As Hashimoto Nobuyuki observed, in our six cities (especially in cities C and E) the owners and operators of agricultural land could make decisions as they wished. Hashimoto suggested that in city E a variety of interests were intertwined in the decisions about drawing the lines (Gyōsei Kanri Kenkyū Sentā 1985: 258). People with large assets preferred to have their land classed as an agricultural zone with low taxes; the brokers who sought capital from financial institutions hoped for an "urbanized" zone designation to raise the collateral value of their land; nurserymen were divided into growers, brokers, and landscapers, and each insisted on his own interests. The important thing was that through these kinds of conflicts, decisions on town zoning were made according to what a majority of the people wanted. Although the administration had issued a "rational plan" before the fact, this plan was not implemented.

The conversion of land in the urbanized zones required only legal notification. But as revealed in our study, even in the urban zones—the areas requiring only notification—each city attended to its own individual characteristics and made its own distinctive response. In order to ensure caution or even pose a barrier to conversion, city A carried out a highly detailed study of actual conditions; city B refused to allow the agricultural council chairperson sole responsibility for receiving the notifications; city D seems to have followed up, at least unofficially, on whether the land was used for the purposes that were announced; city E carried out a prior investigation of all proposed conversions.

With regard to the nonurbanized zones, there was a clearly negative attitude toward requests for conversion in areas with strong farming interests. Areas where desires to farm were weak were tolerant of the conversion. In effect, the intentions of the local residents governed the content of the decisions. By permitting this self-regulation, the agricultural councils gave authority to the people who were directly involved. But one should recognize that this pattern is characteristic of the issue, since the drawing of lines according to the New City Planning Law of 1969 involved the same kind of self-regulation. It is easy for regulation of the interests of highly cohesive groups to result in large measure in recognition of the claims of the groups themselves. Of course, when the interests of others (for example, the residents as a whole) are also articulated strongly and land use plans are debated through procedures (such as local assemblies) that give consideration to these claims, decisions that harmonize multiple, complex interest relationships may well result. But in reality the procedure at present has allowed self-regulation to prevail.

In our understanding of agricultural land conversion, state intentions only set the general direction. Nor is prefectural mediation a large factor. Instead, local-level implementation is carried out through the decisions of the interested parties themselves, guaranteed by the agricultural council system, without great consideration being given to the interests of other parties. Nevertheless, one cannot say that there is no dialogue between the agricultural groups and others. The form of land use is debated not only in zoning and agricultural councils but also as part of the comprehensive planning process in specific municipalities. Other parties can assert their claims during the deliberations of advisory councils and city councils. Therefore, at the next stage research should expand its scope into the comprehensive planning process. But, as noted in regard to city D, because the regional and suburban cities covered in the present study have a high proportion of city council members connected to agriculture, they do not escape completely from the pattern of self-regulation.

A SUGGESTION FOR A NEW CONCEPT
OF LOCAL GOVERNMENT

This book is concerned with the form of local government in the welfare state, which promotes the expansion of governmental functions. As a result of the data presented in chapter 3 and other empirical studies—especially the case studies in this chapter—can we not say that the long-held thesis that welfare states bring about centralization is inadequate? In many cases welfare states rely fundamentally on local governments to implement their programs. In these cases, local conditions are inevitably reflected in the final outcome of the policies. Granted, an increase in programs at the local level that are carried out in concert with the center must be described as centralization. But "centralization" does not always preclude "autonomy." I discussed this point in detail in chapter 3, and it has also been noted recently in studies of central-local relations in other countries (Rose 1984). It is also often pointed out in American studies of Japanese local government (especially in Reed 1982). That is, as implementation theories tell us, local governments transform central plans and policies in accord with their own distinctive conditions.

The local conditions that determine the content of local autonomy include a variety of factors, such as the administrative needs resulting from local demographic structure, the standard of living, the degree of politicization, the support base of the mayor, and the partisan composition of local assemblies. In introducing the system of partial patient payment for medical care of the aged, for example, election promises and the mayor's political commitments played a major role in deciding whether to take measures to alleviate people's financial burdens. In day nursery policy, in contrast, the demographic composition of local society was an important factor in deciding the form of the projects. In the suburbs of large cities the demand for day care was great; moreover, the user groups that could force government to respond to this demand were strong and politically active. In public housing policy, in the metropolitan areas at least, the timing, scale, and form of projects were dependent on municipal initiative. Legally, it was the reverse, but in practice the center proposed and the local areas responded and acted. In agricultural land conversion as well, permits, notifications, and the drawing of boundaries according to the New City Planning Law of 1969 were decided on the basis of such factors as local farmers' cultivation preferences and tax considerations. Therefore, rather than considering reliance of the state on the localities for implementation to be a special feature of welfare services, we should say that it is characteristic of all programs implemented simultaneously by national and local governments. But there are also differences between welfare and agriculture-related programs. Agriculturists are protected procedurally, but they have also organized politically with much success. People involved in public housing or medical care for the aged do not seem to have acquired direct power by increasing their organization or political activism. Their influence seems to be more strongly based on their vote in elections. Therefore, their influence is indirect. The case of day nurseries, with the exercise of great power through the political activity and organization of those involved, resembles the farmers' pursuit of their interests. Thus, day nursery users seem to have different political characteristics from "pure" welfare beneficiaries such as the aged or people with disabilities.

Another important factor is the large role of the prefectures. When the demand for public housing in urban areas lessened, the prefectures took the part of the Ministry of Construction and encouraged the municipalities to apply for assistance. Based on the specific local situations, some prefectures strongly pressed the municipalities, while others did not. Even when municipalities adopted policies of compensating or alleviating people's financial burdens when the national system of partial patient payment was introduced, most were influenced by the policy of the prefectures. In one prefecture in the Kansai area the authorities took a positive stand on compensation; in contrast, prefecture Y (the location of city D of this study) transmitted the state's plan intact to the municipalities. No matter how much the central ministries and agencies would like to effect their own purposes, they have no way to control three thousand municipalities directly. The forty-seven prefectures mediate the state's purposes vis-à-vis the municipalities. Since there are only forty-seven of them, they fit within the state's "span of control." Therefore, state policy cannot help but be influenced by the prefectures that interpret its intent. I would like to end this section with four observations based on our case studies.

First is the relationship between "demands" and "results." We need to define the words. Here, *results* refers to changes in the policy outcome (in the case of day nurseries, this includes the number of establishments, the extent of services provided, and the expansion of service delivery and the decision-negotiation process). *Demands* refers to the needs that can be predicted by objective data (population, number of children, etc.) before they are asserted politically. We can also speak of administratively based demands. Put simply, in public housing, an increase in demands caused an increase in the quantity of policy outcome (in number of buildings). This could be observed in the 1940s, 1950s, and 1960s. After demand decreased in the 1970s, the *mode* of the outcome changed. That is, the number of buildings peaked and the amount of *re*building increased. Another "result" brought about by changes in demand for public housing was a change in political processes and procedures. Concretely, its influence can be seen in every aspect of the central-local bargaining process. In the realm of public housing, we had the spectacle of the Ministry of Construction, acting through the prefectures, actively soliciting "consumption" by the municipalities in urban areas. For their part, the municipalities' attitude toward the Ministry of Construction suggested, "We have lots of requests about other issues too, so could you carry out the renovation of public housing a little more slowly?"

In the case of day nurseries, the decrease in demand—until then focused entirely on facilities—became the stimulus for the adoption of other modes of service. The new modes included extended hours and day nurseries for handicapped children, but these were responses to changes in demand. With regard to medical care for the aged, demand clearly grew rapidly; because the supply of services increased steadily in response, measures were introduced (in the form of the partial payment system) to control the demand itself. The state seems to have realized this goal rather successfully. When we look at central-local bargaining patterns, we don't notice anything particular in the area of day nurseries. But in the case of medical care for the aged, cooperation became necessary as both state guidance and the self-assertiveness of local governments grew stronger.

Second is the question of whether cooperative relationships (often called "policy communities") have formed among the occupational groups that handle the same jobs in administrative units at the three levels. In U.S. and European theories of intergovernmental relations, this is an important concern. We can say that policy community relationships do exist in Japan, but they are different from what has been reported in the United States or Europe. In Japan we do not see an increase in the feeling of belonging to the same profession or the development of common professional or ethical standards. Instead, there is a different kind of mechanism for fostering common interests and concerns among staff members with similar functions at the three levels of the system. It includes detailed communications, the transfer of personnel from the center to the prefectures, and budget hearings held by the central ministries and agencies for the local areas. In these processes the prefecture performs a mediating role; replacing the national government, it supervises the municipalities and participates in their petitioning for subsidized projects. In this context the staff members of local (prefectural and municipal) governments refer to the central ministries and agencies as the "home office." This designation clearly shows their awareness of a hierarchical relationship as well as a feeling of closeness toward colleagues in Tokyo.

Several conclusions emerge from a comparison of policy communities in Japan with those in Europe and the United States. When there is a close relationship between the center and local government, some kind of common tie will inevitably arise from policy area to policy area. However, these common ties contain hierarchical elements in Japan, in contrast to their more egalitarian and professional quality in Europe and the

United States. This kind of theory may appear to reiterate the "Japan as a unique society" theme visible in so much Japanese political, administrative, and social theory, but I think that here the difference between Japan and the West is simply one of degree.

My third observation concerns the influence of urban political dynamics on policy results. Although this is a problem that should be studied further, even from our own study the following may be said. Of our four issue areas, day nursery administration, medical care for the aged, and the conversion of agricultural land seem to reflect the political situation of specific cities. In public housing, however, the implementation of projects is determined more by central-local bargaining than by municipal conditions. When we look at the political conditions of the other three issues, their content varies significantly. The conversion of agricultural land reflects the direct influence on policy decisions of those whose interests are concerned.

Regulatory administration that takes a special class as its object tends to fall under the influence of that class. In the case of conversion of agricultural land, I have already described the influence of agricultural interest groups.

In the administration of day nurseries, the greatest political influence issues from the claims of concerned groups. But their influence is gradually relativized as it is harmonized with other interests at the level of the administrative agency in charge (the child welfare section of city hall) or the mayor's office.

In decisions about alleviating the financial burdens that accompany partial patient payment for geriatric medical care, organizations of the elderly did not influence city governments; instead, initiatives by the mayor or the city administration were significant. But in this case as well, the process was not simply an expression of the mayor's independent thinking; rather, election strategy seems to lurk in the background. Medical care policy should have a great attraction for the older segment of voters, and in city D a connection between elections and the older segment can in fact be observed.

Therefore, we can characterize the political form of each policy area: the conversion of agricultural land is the "self-regulating" type; the administration of day nurseries, the "pressure group" type; and the policies of compensation for geriatric medical, the "electoral" type. In the promotion of public housing in urban areas where there is no internal pressure, municipal administrative bureaus decide that local cooperation in expending the budget will become a bargaining chip in other negotiations with the state (the Ministry of Construction). We might call this the "central bargaining" type of politics.

I have elsewhere taken note of the influence of city councils (Muramatsu and Itō 1986), but in this set of case studies I cannot cite an instance where they played an active role. This is only natural, in the view of traditional theories about the powerlessness of local assemblies in Japanese local government. But because I have hypothesized that city councils do act with authority, I would like to ask why they do not appear here. First, except for public housing, all these cases involve agency-delegated functions. Moreover, because public housing is also a supplementary program, it is closely regulated by the national government; consequently, the councils do not consider it a primary focus for deliberation, and their participation diminishes. But since the other three programs all have independent parts, they become the objects of budget debate. Therefore, we can say that the present study missed its mark by being inattentive to this factor. In fact, even in this study we found that when day nursery fees were raised in city C, there was criticism from the opposition parties in the council; that the administrator in charge of day care in city D enlisted the city council to support his opposition to pressure from the parents' association; and that in city C the issue of university construction was discussed in the council in relation to the conversion of agricultural land. But the role of the councils certainly was not very clear in our present study.

Fourth, and finally, let me summarize the impact of the political process amid the financial distress following the Second Rinchō—excluding the conversion of agricultural land (which did not involve expenditures). In the case of public housing, the total budget decreased and therefore the amount allotted to the prefectures also decreased, but there does not seem to have been any observable change at the level of the individual cities. Day nurseries and medical care for the aged clearly felt the impact of the state's financial distress. Under the influence of the Second Rinchō report, partial patient payment for geriatric medical care was established as part of the Health Care Law for the Aged of 1982. But even though they recognized that the policy of free medical care for the aged contained a number of problems at the municipal level, cities A, D, and F were determined to adhere to the policy of offsetting part of the people's financial burdens for the time being. Thus at the municipal level financial distress did not change the policy of free medical care for the aged. It is interesting to ask where the difference between national and municipal attitudes came from. A variety of factors—such as the fact that the municipalities are the governments interacting directly with the citizens and the fact that during this period the municipalities were relatively well financed—seem to be involved. In the administration of day nurseries, on the other hand, we can see the influence of financial distress as the municipalities gradually turned over day care programs to the private sector and began to raise fees when they encountered difficulties. City E, especially, wrestled with a revision of fees as one element of a citywide plan to rationalize finances. Or, to be more precise, it seized this opportunity to correct a problem that had been pending for a long time.

From what I have just said, control of local government by the center in Japan, as in other countries, has the following characteristics:

1. In special cases, the state can persuade local governments by adopting (or threatening) sanctions, but even though local governments bear the standards established by the center in mind most of the time, they tend to make them reflect local conditions as much as possible. Local governments tend to relax the eligibility requirements the center has set for receiving services and to "improve" the extent of the services.

2. The mediating role of the prefectures is considerable. Because, as mediators, the prefectures' views reflect their own political situations, it is a mistake to overemphasize "orders" from Tokyo. The prefectures differ greatly in their responses to the plans and policies of the center.

3. While the three levels are independent of one another, they promote their programs by exchanging opinions and information, so that the center does not simply decide. The prefectures in particular have of late tended to make their own independent interpretations of the state's plans based on their own individual political situations, and at the same time to initiate independent plans more frequently.

As these tendencies grow stronger in both prefectures and municipalities, conflicts between the two will probably become more common. This is an important factor for the center to take into consideration when it formulates its local strategies. Perhaps as a result of these tendencies, the state has had to give concessions to the prefectures and therefore to the municipalities to the extent that the prefectures have reduced its influence on the municipalities. Rather than guide, the center has to use more direct financial sanctions. And when the municipalities have projects they would like to put into effect, even though they know they are challenging the center, they are willing to accept financial sanctions and still pursue their independent course. Ashford (1986) has pointed out that "the margins" gradually influence the content of policy, and we have observed the same in a number of cases in Japan. Finally, in regard to the previous discussion of professional communities, professionals in the United States and other countries play a large part in the allocation of social benefits (Milnor 1984), but in Japan we cannot see such a prominent role for professionals. Rather, it is the "discovery of politics" at the local level that is the main theme of the present study.

Central Government Subsidies

In the first section, we considered how programs in which the central government participates reflect local conditions as they are implemented at the municipal level. Specifically, we observed that local areas have an independent political structure, which is inevitably reflected in implementation. In the local administrative routine, operating rules—usually generated at the level of the section chief—arise from the circumstances surrounding particular projects. Local section heads' generalized grasp of the situation is transmitted vertically to the related prefectural or central bureau, with which they are linked in a single "policy community" or "functional community." In short, administrative needs that are recognized at the lowest level of implementation are absorbed by the municipalities through their political and administrative mechanisms and transmitted to the prefectures and the center. In addition, as the need arises, members of the local political elite, such as mayors and assembly members, put pressure on state agencies, sometimes directly and sometimes through their locally elected Diet members. We have already seen this process in the case of the governors; in this section I will describe it in relation to the mayors.

The focus of the study introduced below is subsidies. The administration of subsidies is a separate issue from the kinds of central-local relations it leads to (such as the decline of local autonomy), but using a set of questions that mix the two issues, the Chihō Gyōsei Sōgō Kenkyū Sentā in 1979 carried out a nationwide opinion survey of five municipal groups: (1) mayors and deputy mayors, (2) financial section chiefs, (3) social welfare section chiefs, (4) agriculture and forestry section chiefs, and (5) public works section chiefs. The survey was planned by Yonehara Junshichirō (Chihō Gyōsei Sōgō Kenkyū Sentā 1981).

Certainly, subsidies are an effective tool for the control of local governments by the center. For example, because the national government, through a revision of the Sewer System Law, introduced a subsidized "watershed-based sewer system" that promised more favorable conditions, municipalities in the midst of plans for community sewer systems shifted toward the new system and discontinued their old ones. The watershed-based sewer system aimed at taking advantage of economies of scale by incorporating a number of local governments' joint projects, but at the same time the state (the Ministry of Construction) tried to elicit prefectural participation. The policy of reducing agricultural acreage also used subsidies as its primary tool. I cannot here even begin to enumerate the instances where the center used subsidies as inducements to local governments.

Despite these examples of central guidance, when we observe the activities of local governments, the state does not seem to have undermined local autonomy to the extent sometimes asserted. Perhaps, in fact, the strings that come from the center with subsidies are not all that strong, and may well be growing weaker.

When a central bureaucratic system, having successfully engineered modernization, attains moral hegemony, it enjoys independence and discretion; therefore, the vertical administrative control model is appropriate (Tarrow et al. 1978). However, once it is felt that "catch-up modernization" has been accomplished, the moral hegemony of the center recedes, and local demands for benefits from the center become vigorous. Couldn't this process provide a clue to the characteristics of supplementary programs? I think that as the legitimacy and justification of the center gradually weaken, local governments begin to reject central leadership and insist instead on their own autonomy. In the eyes of local governments, perhaps it is desirable for regions to develop economically, through the market, and policies promoting this goal come first. Only if this is not possible do they try to achieve development through public investment by both the local and the central government.

At this stage, it becomes difficult for the central ministries and agencies to control local governments with subsidies. The example of the public housing program in the first section is typical: first, the center has lost its moral hegemony; second, the basic demands of local governments have already been fulfilled, and consequently it is not so simple for a plan conceived at the center to be accepted. When local participation by the center, which previously possessed the authority of a successful catch-up modernizer, becomes unnecessary, what becomes important is the state's presentation of information or suggestions to local governments based on truly rational calculations. If this occurs, the center comes to play, not the role of the regulator who indicates a fixed course, but rather the role of the technocrat.

DO YOU REALLY THINK YOU WANT A SUBSIDY?

The first thing one should ascertain about national subsidies is whether local governing bodies want these subsidies or, conversely, whether they think they are being pressured to accept the subsidies. Then we should ask whether there is an amenability to subsidies in the local budgetary process; if so, is it felt that the national government is controlling local governments through the subsidy? Tables 23, 24, and 25 present data on these points. According to table 23, in response to the question "Do you actively seek national subsidies?" the mayors and their assistants replied distinctly in the affirmative. When other officials were asked to evaluate the activity of the mayors and their assistants ("Are the mayor and his assistants actively seeking subsidies?"), they gave roughly the same responses.

Table 24, which asks whether there are links to the center in local budget decisions, suggests one of the following interpretations. First, it is possible that local governments are dragged into making decisions by the availability of central government subsidies. If local budgets are dominated by subsidized items (tables 24 and 25), that is evidence to support this interpretation. In fact, because a mayor's achievements in his locality are still measured by the size of his budget and the amount of subsidies he has acquired, subsidies certainly can be a tool for the central government to control local areas. The data in table 24 support this interpretation.

The second interpretation, while agreeing that subsidies can become tools of the center for local control, argues that local governments can also exhibit independence in selecting subsidized projects. The idea is that local governments go "shopping," choosing from among all the subsidized programs those that agree with their own aims (Muramatsu and Aqua 1980). All subsidized programs are not pressed equally on local governments, and local governments inevitably must select projects that agree with local conditions, but in any case they can choose.

When a subsidized project has been selected by a local government, it is natural for those in charge of the budget to give it priority as well. I

Table 23 *Eagerness to Acquire Subsidies*

Officials	Always	Usually	Not Always	Never	No Answer	N
Mayor and assistants	68	25	4	0	2	99
Financial section heads	73	19	5	1	1	99
Social welfare section heads	68	20	3	0	8	99
Agriculture and forestry section heads	63	21	3	0	12	99
Public works section heads	86	12	0	0	1	99

QUESTIONS: Mayors and assistants were asked about their own actions: Do you actively seek national subsidies?

The section heads were asked to evaluate the mayor's activities in acquiring appropriations: In your city, are the mayor and his assistants actively seeking national subsidies?

Table 24 *Reliance on National Subsidies*

Officials	Always	Usually	Not Always	Never	No Answer	N
Financial section heads	29	58	11	0	1	99
Social welfare section heads	42	40	10	1	6	99
Agriculture and forestry section heads	39	42	7	0	11	99
Public works section heads	73	23	2	0	1	99

QUESTION: In preparing the budget in your city, do you think priority is given to activities that are assured of receiving national subsidies?

Table 25 *Allowance for National Subsidies*

Officials	Yes	Occasionally	Not Necessarily	Never	No Answer	N
Financial section heads	4	13	27	54	1	99
Social welfare section heads	2	10	23	58	6	99
Agriculture and forestry section heads	3	2	10	73	11	99
Public works section heads	3	5	18	72	1	99

QUESTION: In preparing the budget in your city, do budgetary requests for activities that are assured of receiving national subsidies ever fail to pass?

think it is possible to apply the second interpretation to table 24, although this interpretation presupposes the following two points: (1) each local government selects its subsidized projects independently from among several available, and (2) in the process of executing subsidized projects, it is possible to alter program contents to contribute even more benefits to the local government itself. With regard to the first point, it is fairly basic for each local government to try to acquire the projects it thinks desirable through its locally elected Diet members. When local desires are transmitted to the center through politicians (Diet members), the central government cannot neglect them. As a result, these desires are usually accepted by the central ministries and agencies, and in the end they broaden the scope of the national budget. With regard to the second point, there are countless cases like the attempts to use subsidies for agricultural irrigation ditches to build drainage ditches in newly urbanized areas, but we can also cite the case studies in the first section of this chapter.

THE INFLUENCE OF SUBSIDIES ON LOCAL ADMINISTRATION

How do the people in charge of local administration ward off the influence of subsidies? The attitudes of local officials provide information about which of the above two interpretations is correct. We have already noted the oft-cited "vertical administration" and "micromanagement," and the responses in table 26 indicate an awareness of vertical interference—roughly 60 percent of all groups agreed "completely" or "generally" that there were adverse effects. However, we are interested in attitudinal differences among officials, and there are differences among the administrative groups in their choices of these two responses. In table 26, the percentage of agriculture and forestry section chiefs, social welfare chiefs, and public works section chiefs who felt that vertical administration was harmful was fairly small. It was greater among mayors, their deputy mayors, and financial section chiefs, who were responsible for coordinating the plans of the counterpart agency, often called *Genka* ("home section"), in the central ministry. Thus a simple evaluation of vertical administration is not possible.

When asked if the restrictions imposed by the national government were too detailed for administration under local conditions, the five groups all tended to respond that this was so (table 27). Differentiating between responses, "completely agree" was frequent among social welfare section chiefs and agriculture and forestry section chiefs. The other

Table 26 *Adverse Effects of Vertical Administration*

Officials	Yes	Generally Yes	Not Necessarily	Not at All	No Answer	N
Mayor and assistants	28	46	22	1	2	99
Financial section heads	24	56	18	0	1	99
Social welfare section heads	26	35	30	1	7	99
Agriculture and forestry section heads	16	39	29	2	13	99
Public works section heads	20	44	30	4	1	99

QUESTION: It is said that, because of national subsidies, a vertical administration is in effect in Japan. Have you actually incurred any adverse effects from such an administration?

Table 27 *Restrictive Effects of Government Regulations That Accompany Subsidies*

Officials	Completely Agree	Generally Agree	Not Necessarily	Do Not Agree	No Answer	N
Mayor and assistants	29	51	17	0	2	99
Financial section heads	29	49	20	0	1	99
Social welfare section heads	37	43	12	1	6	99
Agriculture and forestry section heads	43	36	6	3	11	99
Public works section heads	28	46	21	3	1	99

QUESTION: It is said that state restrictions on the execution of subsidized programs are so detailed that it becomes impossible to administer them in accord with local conditions. How do you evaluate this statement?

three groups tended toward "generally agree." Each response reflects the characteristics of the related central ministry or agency.

But when they were asked if the state-specified conditions for execution of nationally subsidized programs were technically superior (table 28), most social welfare section chiefs and agriculture and forestry section chiefs responded negatively, in contrast to the response of public works section chiefs that they were "mostly" superior. In public works, performance is based on a knowledge of engineering and science, and in this field central ministries and agencies with outstanding technical staffs would probably be seen as superior. In contrast, the administrative

Table 28 *Technological Benefits of National Subsidies*

Officials	Always	Usually	Not Necessarily	Never	No Answer	N
Social welfare section heads	1	26	51	11	10	99
Agriculture and forestry section heads	3	28	52	4	12	99
Public works section heads	4	53	40	1	1	99

QUESTION: Do you think that the state-specified conditions for the execution of nationally subsidized programs are technically superior?

Table 29 *Hindrance of Local Operations by National Subsidies*

Officials	Completely Agree	Generally Agree	Not Necessarily	Disagree	No Answer	N
Mayor and assistants	13	28	55	6	2	99
Financial section heads	2	31	59	5	2	99
Social welfare section heads	4	18	61	10	6	99
Agriculture and forestry section heads	5	16	55	12	11	99
Public works section heads	4	21	58	15	1	99

QUESTION: Do you agree that national subsidies hinder the independent administrative and financial operations of local government?

knowledge that is necessary for social welfare and agriculture and forestry section chiefs is a performative knowledge that requires value judgments and an understanding of local people's circumstances, and in which the state ministries and agencies are not necessarily superior.

The above suggests that local bodies are powerfully influenced by the national subsidy system and that influence appears in the form of vertical administration; there is also a feeling that, with all the strings attached to subsidies, a type of administration is imposed that is inappropriate to actual conditions. But when they were asked, at the macro level, if "national subsidies hinder the independent administrative and financial operations of local government," all administrative groups responded negatively (table 29). If table 29 can be considered an expression of opinions about the general framework of central-local relations, then the claims against the central government indicated in tables 26 and 27 appear minor and unrelated to the independence of local financial and administrative operations.

According to those who argue that the subsidy system is necessary, it would be impossible to get local governments to carry out national goals if there were no subsidies. It would be impossible to control the local governments using only the law.

How do local governments respond to this kind of argument? In our study we asked directly: "The central government argues that, if there were no national subsidies, local governments would not discharge their legally defined duties. Is this really so?" (table 30). Almost all administrative groups answered "no." The argument of the national government cited in this question implies that the central government mistrusts local government. In contrast, table 30 indicates that local governments feel it is their own independent responsibility to implement the law. Admittedly, the question is a leading one.

I would like to consider what the various data in this section indicate about the state's frequently mentioned mistrust of local government. We asked: "Recently, the national government has talked about reducing national subsidies. If these subsidies come to an end, should local governments cease the implementation of these programs?" (table 31). Here, too, all the groups responded that they should not. This response is a confirmation by local authorities that central policies, even if induced by subsidies, are ultimately necessary for local governments. And, conversely, that the state provided subsidies for programs that either it or the local governments would somehow have to carry out anyhow.

Mistrust of local government is not just a question of whether local governments will or will not implement the important policies the center wants; it is also a statement about the mode and quality of implementation. Central bureaucrats often say that the capabilities of local governments leave a great deal to be desired. Therefore, the center establishes elaborate procedures for applying for subsidies. However, an analysis of this kind of micromanagement seems to reveal a different way of thinking from that of the past. The state was previously preoccupied with waste and has imposed uniformity throughout the country. But now, when a certain degree of interregional variation is desirable to reflect local conditions, there is no room for change. It is not bad for the

Table 30 *Necessity to Local Operations of National Subsidies*

Officials	Completely So	Generally So	Not Necessarily	Not So	No Answer	N
Mayors and assistants	3	7	48	38	3	99
Financial section heads	0	6	49	43	1	99
Social welfare section heads	4	9	47	33	6	99
Agriculture and fores- try section heads	5	7	45	29	13	99
Public works section heads	2	6	49	40	2	99

QUESTION: The central government argues that, if there were no national subsidies, local governments would not discharge their legally defined duties. Is this really so?

Table 31 *Effect of Cessation of National Subsidies on Local Operations*

Officials	Definitely Yes	Mostly	Not Necessarily	Definitely Not	No Answer	N
Mayor and assistants	7	18	68	4	2	99
Financial section heads	9	20	65	3	2	99
Social welfare section heads	7	15	54	17	6	99
Agriculture and fores- try section heads	5	24	53	6	11	99
Public works section heads	13	16	48	20	2	99

QUESTION: Recently, the national government has talked about reducing national subsidies. If these subsidies come to an end, should local governments cease the implementation of these programs?

center to make an effort to stay cognizant of the local scene. And one may argue that the virtue of Japanese administration lies in the high quality of the teamwork of central and local governments. But in the future there is room for rethinking the relationship and balance between the state and local governments. Rather than an administration of high but uniform quality, we should seek an administration whose content is responsive to local conditions.

As a whole, the responses are consistent. Between the data of table 30 and table 31 there are some discrepancies, but I suspect that table 30 contains "correct" answers, whereas table 31 is more indicative of real intentions. Thus, when we address the matter head-on, local officials assert that they execute laws with a sense of independent responsibility, no matter whether there are subsidies or not; but even when they consider expenses, few acknowledge that some things would not get done. Real conditions lie behind their awareness that they must execute policies even if there are no subsidies. Specifically, it would be very difficult politically to discontinue the programs, inasmuch as they are tied to the support and demands of certain client groups. For each subsidized project, there are invariably clients who will enjoy its benefits.

FROM CATEGORICAL GRANTS
TO GENERAL SUBSIDIES

Finally, let us examine a group of questions concerning reform of the present subsidy system.

In Japan there are two kinds of financial aid from the national government to local governments: the regional transfer tax and national treasury expenditures. The aim of the first is equalization of financial disparities between rich and poor areas; therefore, the way such funds are to be spent is not specified but left to the discretion of the local governments. They are an independent financial resource. The second type provides financial aid in response to applications based on the needs of local governments; the way these subsidies are to be spent is specified accordingly. Because the central government involves itself in each individual program as the numbers and amounts of subsidies grow, the general view is that an increase in specific subsidies harms local autonomy. Because individualized subsidies are handed down vertically from state ministries and agencies without central coordination, they fragment local administration and exacerbate the problem of sectionalism. For this reason, many who argue from the perspective of local government say that individualized subsidies should be reduced and general transfer payments should be increased. At least, in terms of local benefit, regional transfer taxes or general subsidies with few use restrictions are best. In this sense, the "block grants" referred to below can be considered general grants.

For example, Takayose Shōzō (1978: 45), speaking from a practitioner's perspective, says the following about reforming the subsidy system:

First, there is the incorporation of subsidies into transfer taxes. In a word, subsidies are national treasury expenditures; they include both pure subsidies and "financial obligations." The amount of the financial obligations is overwhelmingly larger. Financial obligations are systematic obligations of the national treasury that are determined by law; it may be possible to reduce them, but they cannot be abolished. Livelihood maintenance support is a typical example. Therefore, it is a mistake to think of the reduction of subsidies that promote specific policies and the reduction of systematic financial obligations as being on the same dimension. Even if we talk about "adjusting" subsidies, subsidies that promote specific policies represent a very small piece of the budget. Therefore, unless we incorporate subsidies into the regional transfer tax, there is no possibility of radically reducing their nominal amount.

Takayose makes a number of points, but here I would like you to consider his assertion that the government should reduce subsidies and increase regional transfer taxes by the same amount. The demands of the National Association of Governors and the National Association of City Mayors are at one with this assertion.

The proposal to move from specified subsidies to transfer taxes and block grants is favored in many Japanese local government studies. Is it also favored in the real world? The tables below present the attitudes of the administrative groups in our study toward choices from a "menu" of specific subsidies (table 32), block grants (table 33), and regional transfer taxes (table 34).

Opinions are somewhat divided according to administrative group. On the whole, the respondents tended to support transfer taxes and block grants, but they were divided over the "menu" approach.

Financial section heads were the most supportive of block grants. In three of the groups more than 50 percent approved of such general transfers, albeit with some differences, but 50 percent of the social welfare section chiefs disapproved.

As we see in table 34, mayors and their vice mayors and financial section chiefs tended to approve of transfer taxes, while chiefs of line sections (those sections, such as social welfare, with direct implementation duties) tended to be less enthusiastic, with social welfare chiefs actually disapproving by a small margin.

What interpretation of these data is appropriate? First, to what extent do local government authorities support the regional transfer tax format? The answer is, about half. This figure may be high, but it is certainly not as high as popular opinion would have it. It is unusual, given the prevailing opinion in the scholarly world, where local grants are deemed beneficial for local autonomy. Second, when we analyze different administrative groups, mayors and their assistants and financial section heads tend

Table 32 *Choice among National Subsidies*

Officials	Definitely Yes	Generally Yes	Not Necessarily	Definitely Not	No Answer	N
Financial section heads	2	35	43	17	2	99
Social welfare section heads	14	34	38	5	8	99
Agriculture and fores- try section heads	8	40	37	2	12	99
Public works section heads	18	34	38	5	4	99

QUESTION: Is it desirable to offer local governments a "menu" of national subsidies from which to choose?

Table 33 *Block Grants*

Officials	Definitely Yes	Generally Yes	Not Necessarily	Definitely Not	No Answer	N
Financial section heads	28	45	21	2	3	99
Social welfare section heads	12	27	44	6	10	99
Agriculture and fores- try section heads	18	33	30	3	15	99
Public works section heads	14	37	41	3	4	99

QUESTION: Do you think a system of block grants is desirable?

Table 34 *National Subsidies or Transfer Taxes?*

Officials	Completely Agree	Generally Agree	Not Necessarily	Dis- agree	No Answer	N
Mayor and assistants	24	33	36	4	2	99
Financial section heads	24	40	31	3	1	99
Social welfare section heads	17	29	40	7	6	99
Agriculture and fores- try section heads	17	32	31	7	12	99
Public works section heads	21	33	41	3	1	99

QUESTION: Do you agree with the claim that, from now on, local financial resources should be increased through the regional transfer tax rather than national subsidies?

to come out more strongly for block grants than do people in charge of line sections. Mayors and deputy mayors and financial section heads feel that general block grants enlarge the scope of their discretion. The sections involved in program implementation are comparatively satisfied with the status quo.

In principle, block grants conform to the aims of local government, which center on autonomy. But when one thinks about the actual conditions that general block grants create, they are not necessarily all that is claimed. For example, it is predicted that, as a result of general block grants, the relationship of each line section with its corresponding central ministry and agency will be weakened. As a result, it will be harder for these sections to make use of the technical skills and information of the ministries and agencies. In addition, there might be pressure for changes in the status of the line sections within the organization of city hall. With the end of centrally subsidized programs, financial authorities in local governments will not necessarily continue to give out the same shares of the budget as before. The operational sections will have to devise survival strategies. Until now, the project sections have been able to find support for their activities in their related ministries and agencies even more than in the local government. The reverse side of this is that mayoral calls for regional transfer taxes can be read as claims for consolidating their own organizational leadership. And, for the people at the top, there is often a gap between their own policies and the subsidized program system of the central ministries and agencies. In maintaining alliances with the support groups in their regions, general block grants are more convenient. In sum, while the responses to the question of individual subsidies or general block grants are related to three political dimensions—central-local relations, local politics, and politics within the organization (Kume 1984)—they differ depending on one's point of view.

From an analysis of the above data, we can say the following:

1. Local opinions about subsidies for local governing bodies are not as unified concerning independent sources of funding, regional transfer taxes, or general block grants as the expressions of the National Association of City Mayors or the National Association of Governors suggest. A variety of ways of thinking are possible, and opinions especially vary depending on which "home section" is looking at the issue.

2. Local governing bodies try to obtain as many subsidies as possible; to this extent, they are induced to support national policies. But a

high proportion of local officials say that, whether subsidies influence the policies and implementation of local government
or not, they do not hinder their autonomous functioning. On this
point, however, opinions are divided between line section chiefs
on the one hand and top officials and financial section chiefs on the
other.

3. We have really not addressed this point adequately, but when
we look at population size, we see that the bigger the local government unit, the less it feels the influence of subsidies (Chihō
Gyōsei Sōgō Kenkyū Sentā 1981).

There is a problem in how to interpret data that present an apparent contradiction: as a whole, subsidies seem to be effective in inducing
local governments to carry out national policies, but at no loss of local
autonomy.

Perhaps the explanation is that state subsidies are often for programs
that have been established as a result of local government hearings, and
local governments therefore do not feel that unnecessary measures are
being forced upon them. In other words, subsidies do not undermine
autonomy. In fact, the respondents tended to think that even if state subsidies were discontinued, local governments should pick them up and
continue them. I think we should try to accept at face value the responses
of local government administrators that assert their autonomy. Their
dissatisfaction with subsidies is with the amounts and methods involved
(Kyōdō Tsūshinsha 1982: 88).

It is interesting that there are slight differences of opinion about autonomy between mayors and financial section heads on the one hand
and those in charge of line sections on the other. The mayors and the
financial section heads think that transfer taxes and block grants are better than categorical grants, but few line section heads agree. This difference parallels the opposing views of the Ministry of Home Affairs and
the other ministries and agencies.

At the same time, the position of people who work in the same policy
arenas has become the basis for identical viewpoints and common feelings, whether in the central or the local government. It is possible that
to some degree the "professional communities" that I described hypo-
thetically above have materialized. These common feelings and identity
of views suggest a sort of collegial professionalism. As a matter of local
governmental dynamics, the image of intergovernmental relations be-

comes one of coordinating/regulative/staff functions versus operational/line functions.

Thus, one of the conclusions of the second section of this chapter—that the essence of local government does not lie only in its relationship to the center but must also be seen as a local process—becomes an overall emphasis of this book. And I would like to add an evaluative comment on state subsidies. This section has argued only that the common thesis that subsidies serve to control local government is too simple. But if we look at the results in other countries of turning local subsidies into general block grants, we do not find that general grants are some wonderful practice about which no one complains. Theodore Lowi argues that in the U.S. experience (in the revenue-sharing system of the Nixon administration) local governments used this newly offered revenue source to pay the salaries of public officials and repay loans, not to confront their truly serious administrative needs (1981: 191–95). This finding suggests that subsidies in general are necessary as a mechanism to get local governments to implement truly necessary national policies.

CHAPTER 5

A Reexamination of the
Concept of Local Government

The Three Stages of Local Government

Japanese local government has passed through three stages; in discussing them, I would like to present a hypothesis about the development of autonomy. In the first stage, the central bureaucracy, freely using the administrative system (agency-delegated functions), the financial system (subsidies and the regional transfer tax), and the personnel system (moving central government officials into local government), created an integrated structure of centralized central-local relations. During the second stage, the central ministries and agencies used this integrated structure to seek local cooperation under the banner of economic growth, and the local governments responded. It was an era of regional development. The structure created in the first period was still functioning, but simply following the orders of the state was not sufficient for regional development in the second stage. Local governments had to proceed in accord with their own active plans; consequently, it became more and more important for the localities to formulate their own political purposes. They became concerned with such regional questions as whether to work toward development, to what extent, and how. For example, a group of Diet members based in agricultural villages succeeded in introducing the "correction of regional income differences" as one target of the Comprehensive National Development Plan. But this kind of activity was really designed to reflect the political purposes of development plans already existing in local government. And we have seen how, when the "new industrial cities" were being designated, each local government tried to use whatever political power it had to be nominated. At this stage local governments seem to have become politicized to a considerable extent. The third stage is characterized by the proliferation of leftist local governments and citizens' movements against pollution in the late 1960s and early 1970s. It was a period when local governments became highly politicized and confronted the state. Leftist-dominated governing bodies accumulated a record of achievement in their prevention of pollution and their promotion of social welfare. But the "confrontation" of this period should not be construed too narrowly. It was highlighted by that between central conservatives and local leftists, but—more important—in confronting the center, local governments of all persuasions discovered that they were capable of opposing the state.

During this third period, then, local governments began to assert themselves by making more claims against the center, regardless of whether they had conservative or progressive mayors. In order to assert themselves in opposition to the center, they needed sufficient political resources. And beginning in the late 1960s Japanese local governments began to accumulate them. But political resources are meaningless if they merely exist. They do not become political resources until they are discovered and used. For example, beginning in the late 1960s locally elected Diet members became a resource that local governments could use. Previously, locally elected Diet members had been important for transmitting local interests to the center, but because the ruling Liberal Democratic Party was enlarging its policy-making power at this time in relation to the bureaucracy, they became an even more useful political resource. Nevertheless, unless aware of this possibility, local governments could not use them. A characteristic of political resources is that, unless people use them skillfully, they cannot be transformed into real power. Politics is an art.

What I am trying to say is that, beginning in the late 1960s, local governments were able to accumulate both political resources and the techniques for using them. It was the leftist governing bodies that made the most use of this potential, but during this period local governments in general began, when the necessity arose, to persist in their claims against the center. In the mid-1960s urban public needs such as environmental, welfare, and consumer issues came to be felt acutely by local governing bodies, and the number of demands from the local governments upon the center increased dramatically. This reflected local governments' growing awareness of their influence and resources, and their conscious use of them. On the one hand local governments found themselves in the middle of a trend toward centralization, as we saw in the increase in agency-delegated and subsidized functions; on the other hand, they were moving to broaden their autonomy.

We can see the increase in agency-delegated and subsidized functions as an indication of centralization, but I would like to ascertain whether my observation of the enlargement of local autonomy is correct. I have a hypothesis that the extent of local influence on the state is proportionate to the extent of local politicization. I arrived at this hypothesis indirectly. First, it emerged vaguely in an article (Muramatsu 1975c) on the three stages of development of postwar Japan's local government summarized above, but it was made explicit by Ronald Aqua in his statement, "The more partisanship expands, the more autonomy and independence expand," in his analysis of my article in his Cornell University Ph.D. dissertation (1979). When I looked again at Aqua's dissertation, I thought that partisanship was indeed a major factor, but that the explanation for local influence on the state must lie in broader political factors, which include but are not limited to partisanship alone. The idea of "politicization," as noted above, ran throughout this process.

Another thing that needs to be explained in relation to Aqua's statement is whether local politicization enhances autonomy and independence. I stated above that politicization produces an influence in relation to the center, but I did not say that this is the same as autonomy. However, if one basic condition holds—that is, if local governments are intent on autonomous operations—then, according to my hypothesis, the extent of politicization is the most important factor in determining the extent of autonomy. First, *politicization* means that a local government, exposed to a number of political forces, takes political positions. Political partisanship is among the most important factors, but there are differences of degree within the positions of the political parties.

Next, what does *autonomy* mean? It means that local governments themselves manage the collective affairs of the local citizens. In other words, using their own political and administrative mechanisms, localities define their own interests. Previously, legal and other forms of institutional centralization seemed to rob local governments of this kind of autonomy. If we consider the legal system and the structures by which, for example, fiscal resources are allocated, the twentieth century is clearly the era of centralization. Many people say that this situation has led to a reduction of local independence and therefore of autonomy. But the matter is not so simple, as I shall make clear below.

Autonomy and Activity: A Dilemma

In theories of local government in modern states, autonomy and centralization are seen as contradictory.

In an era of centralization, a dilemma is created by demands on local governments to raise levels of activity or service on the one hand and to maintain their independence on the other. Theoretically, local government with elected officials guarantees both adequate services and autonomy. Why is that? No matter how much independence a government has, unless it delivers a certain level of services, it will not fulfill the functions expected of a local government; and no matter how many functions it performs, if they are based entirely on orders from the center, there is no autonomy. In the actual political process it is extremely difficult to have the two together, because achieving one tends to make it hard to achieve the other.

Usually, we consider autonomy to be the product of two functions— of self-steering and self-control, to use Deutsch's (1966) terms. Autonomy is the power of governments to take action based on their own judgment (self-steering) and, using the information they obtain about the results, to correct any mistakes in judgment (self-control). This self-steering and self-control is often called independence (Deutsch 1966). But political autonomy must also be evaluated by whether it achieves its goals. Because it is political, local government must create and implement the policies the citizens want. This is the service aspect of local government. For this, administrative resources are necessary. Many of these resources—capable personnel, authority, funding—are under the control of the state. Of course, in addition to acknowledging the principle of local autonomy, the central government has previously given local governments some degree of authority and financial resources, although usually not enough. Therefore, local governments face the problem of how to marshal the resources necessary to offer the services they think are needed.

Today's citizens are vigorous in making demands. Regardless of whether the central government or local governments have the authority and the means to attain them, citizens tend to demand improved levels of administration. On the other hand, the central government tends to attach conditions when it gives authority and other resources, and to attach strings to funding or a reallocation of the budget. This is part of the logic of the modern state, which concentrates sovereignty in the state. Local governments must constantly choose between independence and level of service. When a country's desire to catch up with Europe and the United States is strong, local governments set aside their differences of opinion with the state, focus on administrative quality, and go along with the state's intentions. But once modernization has been achieved and it becomes unclear how to proceed, voices come forth calling for independence in local government.

In fact, in their activities over the past twenty years, local governments seem to have chosen new administrative functions based on different values from those of the center, or they have given different weights to existing activities. The eruption of leftist local governments around 1970 can be explained as a concomitant of this trend in citizens' concerns.

But as a later problem, when the independence of local government is stressed and the intentions of the center are ignored, local governments have to put up with existing administrative standards and cannot expect aid from the central government in the form of administrative resources. Continuing to stress independence alone is difficult, for citizens are never satisfied with present conditions. And if neighboring municipalities improve their administrative levels, or if standards have to be lowered because of a decrease in tax revenues, the citizens are unlikely to keep silent. In such cases, if a local government clings to its independence, citizens' trust in it will decrease and local autonomy risks becoming a hollow shell. A desire to keep up with neighboring local governments as a mechanism for raising the quality of services has already been explained by the horizontal political competition model. Nevertheless, if local governments choose to raise administrative standards, thus attempting to satisfy the citizens better, they may run the risk of increasing state intervention. That is, there are aspects of independence that are dangerous. The independence described above seems to have more or less the same meaning that "autonomy" traditionally had in local government. Should we not think of the autonomy of these local governments in the same way?

One derives, from an analysis of the contradictory relationship between level of activity or service and autonomy in the traditional sense, the impression that changes are being sought in the concept of auton-

omy. Local government currently exists under conditions where the citizens demand high levels of public services and where the main local administrative resources and legal authority reside in the central government; consequently, autonomy cannot be achieved as it once was, by
escaping from the control of the central government. Therefore, present-
day local government exists within a process where goals are achieved by
bargaining with the central government and by forming cooperative and
confrontational relationships with various social groups. Autonomy still
consists of self-direction and self-control. But the context of direction
and control is not limited to the geographical confines of local governments; it includes the central ministries and agencies, and it inevitably
transcends administration, expanding into the broad political world of
politicians and other actors. The activities of groups outside the governmental structure are also important elements. Present-day autonomy lies
within a social, economic, and political network that has broadened in
complexity. It consists of the assertion of interests by local government
structures, based on the will of local citizens, and the actions designed to
realize those interests. The dilemma of independence and services had
further stimulated the lobbying of the state that accompanies horizontal
political competition.

To return to the issue raised in the first section, in this sense the politicization of local government contributes not only to local influence vis-
à-vis the state but also to the fulfillment of local autonomy. For present-
day local government, which must negotiate and deal with various
political participants, politicization is indispensable; in its absence, it
would be difficult to realize full autonomy.

In the first section, I used the examples of locally elected Diet members' power to elicit benefits and the leftist governing bodies' power to
criticize. Next I would like to suggest that there are, in the essential activities of local governments themselves, factors that enable them to
influence the central government and other actors. As I note in the next
section, this issue is related to the question of what we see as the special
character of the modern state.

Local Government and the Welfare State

As a point of reference I would like here to mention some
trends in local government theory in other countries. In looking at the

twentieth-century welfare state, the British political scientist Richard Rose (1984) has observed an expansion of independence in local governments, noting that it has become possible for local governments to bargain with the center because of the volume of public services that the welfare state delivers. The capacity to bargain is, in the terms we have used, a local government resource. According to Rose, (1) in the administration of service delivery, central and local governments inevitably stand in a relationship of overlapping authority. Another British political scientist, R. A. W. Rhodes (1982), has said that because of its "dependence in implementation," the center inevitably relies on local governments. The important point is that as the welfare state grows, the domain characterized by overlapping authority expands, increasing the importance of local government. But, Rose adds, (2) there are many spheres in which the state treats local government as a subordinate structure. And (3) many policies are advanced by the common intentions of the state and a few related local groups. According to Rose, these three patterns coexist in present-day British central-local relations.

To put Rose's patterns in the context of Japanese political science, (1) the pattern in which responsibility for service delivery gives local governments negotiating strength vis-à-vis the state clearly corresponds to the pluralist perspective; (2) the aspect in which the central government gives orders corresponds to the vertical administrative control model, which is linked to theories of bureaucratic superiority; and (3) the determination of state policy toward localities through the interaction of a small number of organizations and the central government corresponds to corporatism. The next section takes up the theoretical problems that emerge from this linkage of central-local relations to theories of political systems. Even though Rose says that the three categories described above coexist, one characteristic of the modern welfare state is the importance of increased local influence. Therefore we must consider the proposition that the growth of the welfare state increases local influence. The interesting part of Rose's observation is that, even though central-local relations were once discussed as though they involved one center and one locality, actually we should see them as relations between a pluralistic center and a multiplicity of local governments. Moreover, these local governments are independent entities. Therefore, conditions arise in which the central government of a welfare state cannot hope to control all local governments and in which, because local governments are the providers of public services, the state must depend on local governments instead. Only slightly exaggerating in describing the situation,

Rose states that from a service delivery perspective, central government is now the peripheral institution of government (1984: 8).

If we keep the modern states of Europe in mind, we see that Rose's theory suggests that the character of the state has changed. In the modern state—England in this case—central-local relations had a dual structure. That is, the central government engaged in high politics and the local governments engaged in low politics; the two did not have a deep relationship with each other. The center was concerned with law and morality and honor, and problems that arose because of industrialization or urbanization were considered local problems. Here, the coordinate authority model is appropriate (see figure 1 in chapter 1). But two factors appeared in the nineteenth century that complicated this model. The first was the growth of the communications system; the second was the development of the welfare state.

Because I have already discussed the second factor, I shall here touch briefly only on the first. Rose considers the beginning of the postal system to have played a major role in central-local relations. The postal system required a national mail delivery network, and generated activities connecting the center and localities. In other countries, the role of the postal system was played by railroads, highways, or canals. The growth of a national communication network does not allow mutual isolation of central and local governments, and forces them to develop a relationship of overlapping authority.

Thus, as the state evolved into a welfare state that participates actively in society, its character changed dramatically. The effectiveness of state functions has come to depend on a supply system based on national networks. In this way, its control permeates everyday life, but the same process expands the influence of local government vis-à-vis the center.

In Japan, Nishio Masaru has made similar observations, although not necessarily linked to the development of the welfare state. He says:

Even though decisions are made by the country's legitimate representative bodies, unless they are approved by a majority of the community of those with a direct interest in them, it becomes impossible to implement these decisions. Then, because the task of harmonizing and integrating the will of this community is not something that state institutions do well, it turns out that the country relies on the integrative capacity of the prefectures and the prefectures rely on the integrative capacity of the municipalities. Therefore, the power relationship of the national and local governments has been greatly transformed [1979: 256].

Let us return once more to Rose's proposition. He is not simply arguing in favor of the new direction of the welfare state. Rather, he is searching for a balanced theory with which to understand central-local relations. As I have already said, he discusses three patterns of central-local relations. According to Rose, because central-local relations were in the past analyzed almost entirely in legal terms, extreme theories came into being that made no distinction between central and local governments or between governments and private organizations. This is an atomistic pluralistic point of view; in it there is only bargaining between political actors. But according to Rose, we should not carry this line of argument too far. There are cases where the government unilaterally nationalizes private organizations or when it acts to decide the financial possibilities and conditions of private organizations by changing the tax system. That is, we should not exclude the political inequality that exists between the public and the private. At the same time, Rose suggests, the fundamental inequality between central and local governments and their differences in character are not eliminated by the authority of the central government.

The presumption of dependence of the state on local governments, which Rose and Nishio suggest, implies that the interdependence of central and local government will be richly varied. Figure 3 shows four possible patterns. They can be used not only to characterize a country's political system and policy-making process but also to analyze the relationships between central and local governments in various policy areas. The following explains the specific conditions of each pattern:

1. Mutual independence—almost no examples in Japan; previously the relationship between federal, state, and local governments in the United States was thought to follow this pattern.

2. Unilateral dependence of local government on the center—many subsidized programs and agency-delegated functions, which can be understood in terms of the vertical administrative control model.

3. Unilateral dependence of the center on local government—reliance on local government for the implementation of state policies, which can be understood in terms of the horizontal political competition model.

4. Overlapping authority—many of the functions of the welfare state. In Japan there are many examples of this pattern in the shared system where all levels—central, prefectural, and municipal—participate.

Degree of State Dependence on Local Government

		High	Low
Degree of Local Dependence on the State	High	Overlapping authority	Unilateral dependence
	Low	Unilateral dependence	Mutual independence

Figure 3. Patterns of Central-Local Relations. *Source: Adapted from Hanf and Scharpf 1978: 356.*

Relationships of Overlapping Authority

As noted above, there has been an increase in central-local relationships of overlapping authority throughout the world. From the literature on the subject we can see that in Japan as well there has been an increasing need for a horizontal political competition model—in addition to the vertical administrative control model—to understand central-local relations. This section has two themes: a better understanding of the overlapping authority model and a view of the form of local government that exists within relationships of overlapping authority.

Here I would like to take up once more the arguments of Deil Wright cited in chapter 1. Wright (1978: chap. 1) considers three models of central-local relations: the separated, or coordinate, authority model, in which the federal, state, and local governments operate independently of one another; the inclusive authority model, in which the federal government subsumes the state governments and state governments subsume municipal governments; and the overlapping authority model, in which all three are interdependent (see figure 1). Traditionally the United States was considered to fit the coordinate authority model. Because local governments were "the creation of the states" in the United States, the coordinate authority model best portrayed the independence of the federal and state governments and the clear separation of jurisdiction between them. The states were thought to include local governments, and local governments exercised only the authority given to them by the states.

But the New Deal brought the U.S. federal-state relationship closer to the inclusive authority model. Welfare and urban policies were promoted under federal leadership, and even the states were caught up in the widening jurisdictional net of the federal government. Even as the states preserved their independent and broad-scale functions, the overall course of their policies became subsumed by the federal governments. Richard Nixon's new federalism and Ronald Reagan's conservatism, in contrast, moved in the direction of the separated authority model; in this sense they were trying to restore the state governments to their previous form. Generally, the relations among the U.S. federal, state, and local governments have been understood in this way.

But Wright says that the overlapping authority model explains—albeit with a certain amount of wishful thinking—central-local relations in the United States today. While each of the three levels of government possesses spheres that are safe from the interference of the others, they also possess areas of common concern and common responsibility. In some of these common areas all three levels participate; in others, two of the three cooperate. In any case, relationships of overlapping authority emerge among the participating governments in these areas. In Wright's view, in the overlapping authority model the independence of each governmental unit is relatively small (because of its great dependence on other units), and bargaining becomes an important process in the implementation of programs. Wright's overlapping authority model can also be used to understand the relationships among the central, prefectural, and municipal governments in Japan.

From the theory of vertical administration we learn that the interests of the Ministry of Home Affairs and the other central ministries and agencies tend to be in opposition. And in my own horizontal political competition model, I have emphasized that competition among local governments on the same level and among neighboring local governments exerts a major influence on the formation and implementation of policy. But in my research on local assemblies (Muramatsu and Itō 1986) and my observations of change in the concept of special cities, I have learned that, even among local governments, there are differences between prefectures and municipalities and, among municipalities, differences between eleven designated cities (designated by the minister of home affairs based on the Local Government Act) and other cities and towns. Therefore, in order to deepen our understanding of overlapping authority, we must clarify the distinctive positions of the Ministry of Home Affairs, other ministries and agencies, the prefectures, and the municipalities.

The most important work for considering this issue is Amakawa Akira's (1983) "Wide-Area Administration and Local Decentralization" ("Kōiki gyōsei to chihō bunken"). In this essay Amakawa takes the issue of wide-area administration as his starting point and proposes a framework for ordering relations between the central and local governments. His model of central-local relations posits two axes: decentralization-centralization and separation-fusion. Decentralization-centralization refers to the extent to which local governments can decide on their own goals in accord with the intentions of the citizens of their area. In decentralization, local governments can decide their own goals; in centralization, the opposite is true. Separation-fusion refers to the issue of who performs the administrative functions of the state within a locality. Under separation, the organs of the state themselves perform state functions; under fusion, even though certain functions belong to the central government, local governments take partial charge of them within their own area in conjunction with their own functions. This concept of separation differs slightly from the one I have used in this book.

Even in prewar Japan, because local citizens elected mayors and local assembly members, there was considerable decentralization. But the prewar government tended toward fusion, as we can see in the power of the Home Ministry to suppress the individual ministries' and agencies' inclinations toward separation and to turn the prefectures into consolidated local offices of the central government. The key to fusion was the dominant authority of the executive.

Postwar reforms strengthened the trend toward the decentralization end of the centralization-decentralization axis. A different incarnation of the separation-fusion axis was also possible, because the Home Ministry—the key to this axis—was dismantled. But, in fact, fusion was promoted by the postwar Home Affairs Agency (later Ministry). The fusion thus created was incomplete, however, and unable to control the separatist tendencies of the ministries and agencies. The foregoing is also Amakawa's analysis of Japanese central-local relations. His analysis starts from the premise that each actor has its own strategy of conceptualizing the reform of the system. These actors can be divided into four groups: (1) the Ministry of Home Affairs, (2) the other ministries and agencies, (3) the prefectures, and (4) the municipalities (especially the large cities). Each actor, in accordance with its own vested interests, has the inclinations based on past experience presented in figure 4. Each group has its own plans for new systemic reforms and acts to protect its preferences

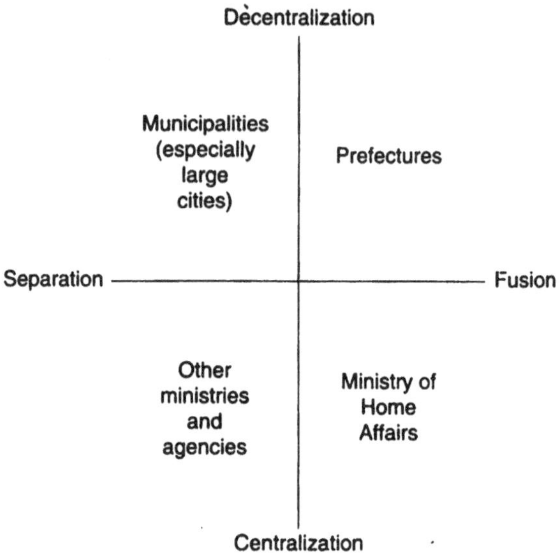

Figure 4. Bureaucratic Politics in Central-Local Relations.

and interests; as a result, they all "converge on the protection of the status quo" (Amakawa 1983).

While Amakawa's theory rests on traditional administration-centered paradigms, he offers a very appropriate sketch of central-local "bureaucratic politics." Amakawa's observations are based on an analysis of the region-wide governmental system proposed in the past forty years. The prefectures tend toward fusion, but regardless of whether they would choose Amakawa's region-wide governmental system, we can see a tendency toward separation in their insistence on the abolition of agency-delegated functions, thus locating the prefectures in the upper right quadrant of figure 4. For example, a Kyōdō News Service survey indicates that local executives want a clear distinction between central and local affairs (Kyōdō Tsūshinsha 1982: 98–105). The notion of separation explains the opposition of the line ministries and agencies with direct implementing responsibilities to the insistence of the prefectures and Ministry of Home Affairs on the devolution of functions to local government, as well as the insistence of the prefectures, versus the central ministries and agencies, that program sharing be abolished. "Separation," as used by the prefectures in opposing ministerially delegated functions, is a bit different from "separation" as defined by Amakawa. It refers to local participation in the line ministries' programs and also to a reduction in state participation in these projects. Generally the separation model of local government found in this book follows this usage.

We must note that the decentralization-centralization axis was originally a political one. Amakawa defines centralization and decentralization in systemic terms, but I think that this pairing is also applicable as a political axis that includes political party activity.

While advocating the horizontal political competition model, I would also argue that in the competition between local governments, locally elected Diet members play a powerful role as advocates of local interests. The more farm villages a region has, the more this is the case. The state relies on the income tax, a wonderfully fungible form of revenue; therefore the state is the target of the rural prefectures in their pursuit of a reallocation of wealth. The parliamentary gerrymandering that favors farming villages ensures effective revenue redistribution in their direction. When local governments petition and lobby the state, their own parliamentary cheerleaders join in, although not all localities are equally matched in this competition. The fierce competition between local governments as a whole becomes a vehicle for communicating local needs to the state and bringing about new policies, but each local government's share of the fruits of these policies is determined by its own competitive strength. It has been suggested that, in the competition between local governments, victories and losses are decided by the power of the local politicians (Hirose 1981); if this is so, then it would be a powerful incentive to individual politicians to redouble their efforts and thus enhance their political stature. Then, where should political parties and politicians be placed in the quadrants of figure 4?

As I have already suggested, political parties and politicians become cheering sections for both prefectures and municipalities, and they also contribute to the separationist form of local control (vertical administration) preferred by the ministries and agencies, which is so conducive to sectionalism. When local politicians become leaders in the ruling party, they are spurred on by the need to demonstrate leadership vis-à-vis local government. If we are to adopt Rose's manner of interpretation, that is, if we are to interpret the order of things solely from the party's point of view, we need to divide party activity into several categories. Before taking up the question of whether the functions of the parties are especially relevant for certain groups, I would like to note that they possess influence that is essential to all the actors in Amakawa's typology. Thus, we can divide the functions of the parties into four categories, according to which group they support:

1. Support for basic local governing bodies. Primarily effective in grabbing a share of the budget, this role is played by the locally elected Diet members of the ruling party.

2. Support for prefectures when they insist on institutional independence. The groups of politicians most likely, for reasons of principle, to play this role are the opposition. But coalitions of key prefectural organizations and opposition parties have appeared only rarely—for example, during the period when Tokyo and Osaka were in the hands of leftist administrations. As for the conservative Diet members—for example, those on the Local Administration Committee of the House of Representatives—they perform the fourth category of functions (see below).

3. Support of groups of politicians for the activities of the ministries and agencies. Here, Diet members connected with various interests (*zoku*) are powerful, but other Diet members also support various ministries by trying, for example, to influence "their" ministry's place in the national budget.

4. Support for the viewpoint of the Ministry of Home Affairs. This kind of activity is exhibited by Diet members during bargaining between the Ministry of Home Affairs and the Ministry of Finance.

I think that the decision-making power in each of these categories depends on the influence that the various political parties and politicians exercise, and in this sense Japan's central-local relations are a politically guided process. At the same time that politics and administration are intertwined at the central and the local levels, there are relationships between local politics and the central administration and between local administrators and central politicians; accordingly, we can see the four linkages among them that are shown in figure 4.

In examining the ideas of the two authors presented above, Wright and Amakawa, I would like to push my hypothesis of interdependence one step further.

In the first place, when we look at the system of legal authority that covers both central and local governments, Wright's overlapping authority model is undeniably appropriate to some aspects of the modes of allocation. In the authority system (i.e., the administrative system) that cuts through Japan's central and local governments vertically, the three levels are bound closely together and share authority and responsibility for a given policy area. Amakawa derived the separation-fusion axis from this fact. The shared or fused aspects of the Japanese system are the polar opposite of the federal-state separatism that Wright sees as characterizing the early federalism of the United States. However, according to Wright, the need arose for a model of overlapping authority in the United States because fused aspects also appeared there after the 1960s.

For a long time, Japanese scholars of public administration somewhat exaggerated the authority of legally superordinate bodies in their models, and they denigrated the autonomous elements of subordinate groups inherent in this authority; consequently, they concluded that the existence of any fused aspects was simply part of the centralized authority. They thus began to argue that Wright's separated authority model was the true model of autonomy. But there are two problems here: there is a real question whether one can leap from the fact that intergovernmental relations are *fused* to the conclusion that they are *centralized*; and these scholars have not addressed the question of whether the idealized separated authority model is adequate to describe a complex, highly industrialized society.

My position, which is close to Amakawa's, is one of "decentralization in fusion." But because Amakawa emphasizes the fused aspects—even though he recognizes such elements of decentralization as popular elections—he seems to say there is little autonomy. And he does not mention the political dynamics by which a decentralized system somehow generates independence in operation. I think, after an empirical analysis of Amakawa's fused aspects (see the first section of chapter 4), that local government can be autonomous. Autonomy is possible *due to* the decentralization (the popular election of local executives and assembly members) cited by Amakawa. I think it is possible to have structural centralization and political autonomy. In order for political autonomy to be possible, local governments must have their own will. And autonomy cannot be achieved unless that will is successfully realized in processes where all the various political actors operate, including the central government. Intergovernmental relations in today's advanced industrial states inevitably have a common legal and financial system. In this sense, they have inherent tendencies toward centralization. The observations of many early-twentieth-century theorists were not mistaken, but if we extend these observations to include political and administrative dynamics, the achievement of political autonomy is possible within structural centralization. Because, as Rose and Wright say, central-local relations overlap (including a certain central administrative dependence on local government), the shared or fused relations involved in administrative functions often become a mechanism by which local governments influence the state. For example, increased demands for day nurseries led local governments to sue the state.

Within overlapping authorities, the key to central-local relations is bargaining. The participants in bargaining are many and varied, as Amakawa suggests. But in addition to distinguishing between the Ministry of Home Affairs, the other central ministries and agencies, the prefectures, and the municipalities, it is important to distinguish between the politicians and groups of administrative officials at the central and the local levels. Politicians are especially powerful in bargaining that moves from below to above, as we saw in tables 11 and 12. (Recent literature such as Hirose 1981 also demonstrates this point.) Those appearing in table 11 are national-level politicians, but the lobbying activities of local assembly members on central politicians play a larger role than is usually thought. Central and local elections are processes that link the center and local governments.

Whether local governments can formulate their own distinct will, as well as how they do this, is a question of the local political structure. Local government is a system of dual representation, consisting of local executives and assembly members, but in actual practice the preeminence of the executive is clear. The "presidential" position of the executive and the tradition of administrative supremacy has even tended to relegate the political activity of local assembly members to "petitioning" the government. But the leadership of the executive is governed by other factors as well. The wishes of local assemblies and their members, heretofore not considered important, play a particularly large role in determining the formulation of executive initiatives (e.g., Muramatsu and Itō 1986). Unless we analyze in detail the factors that determine the actions of these executives, we cannot understand the dynamics of local government—for their actions are determined by the internal processes of local politics.

I have argued that central-local relations are relations of overlapping authority, that the key to them is an understanding of the bargaining process, and that many local government strategies in bargaining can be explained by the principle of competition between local governments. Within this model, what position is occupied by the intermediate body of the prefecture? In their relations with most municipalities, the prefectures act as referees in the intermunicipal competition over specific projects, and sometimes they act as supporters for lobbying by the municipalities for decisions at the national level. In addition, they execute their own programs. For these programs, the administrative standards of other prefectures and of municipalities within their own boundaries become important. The prefectures also are of a competitive mind. But their larger role is that of an intermediary body. We must look for an integrated description of central-local relations that weaves together the elements of politics and administration, of prefectures and municipalities, and — at the central level — of the Ministry of Home Affairs and the other ministries and agencies.

Pluralism and Corporatism

When we observe local politicization and the resulting expansion of local influence on the center and opening up of possibilities for local autonomy — that is, when the role of local government grows large within the political system as a whole — it becomes necessary to consider how this kind of theory relates to broader theories of the political system. As I have already suggested, this issue is related to the theories of pluralism and corporatism.

Pluralism argues, in direct contrast to theories of monolithic, unitary power structures, that power is dispersed among a large number of actors. Robert Dahl (1966), the father of pluralist theory, posited municipalities and middle-level local governments (the states in the United States) as an element in this kind of pluralist structure, but recently political scientists have appeared who argue, within a comparison of pluralism and corporatism, for a specific link between local government and the political system. The English scholar R. A. W. Rhodes is one of these (see Muramatsu 1986 [Japanese]). In addition, Richard Samuels (1983) has carried out an empirical analysis of policy formation in Japan's local governments for the purpose of theorizing about Japan's political system. Thus, the need has arisen to analyze theories of local government within a larger framework.

In order to carry out the task described above, Samuels conducted a painstaking case study and compiled survey data on local government officials. Particularly interesting is his systematic framework for central-local relations. As table 35 shows, he divided the institutional forms of

Table 35 *The Structure of Central-Local Relations*

Linkage Type	Direction of Flow	
	Horizontal	*Vertical*
Intergovernmental	Egalitarian	Tutelary
Extragovernmental	Interorganizational	Intraorganizational
Integrative	Pluralist	Corporatist

SOURCE: Adapted from Samuels 1983: 17.

central and local relations into intergovernmental and extragovernmental relations. Intergovernmental relations refer to links among the various activities of government units that preside over different geographical units. These include relations between local governments and also between local governments and the center. Extragovernmental relations include power relations where local governments are affected from the outside by, for example, private-sector actors and activities where local governments try to exert their influence in relation to higher or broader dimensions of the political system. The efforts of business or labor to influence the decisions of mayors and the efforts of local politicians to influence the national-level activity of political parties are examples of this. Samuels also distinguishes—looking horizontally across table 35, at the determination of benefits for local government—between those determined independently (horizontally) and those determined by the national government (vertically). Samuels notes, as I have argued above, that previous interpretations of Japanese local government have had a vertical bias. He points out that the horizontal elements were obscured by this bias and attempts to redress the balance, an attempt with which I strongly concur. Moreover, he successfully analyzes extragovernmental relations and activities, as shown in table 35, by collecting information, beginning with a case study of the Tokyo Bayshore Highway, to survey data concerning the attitudes of local civil servants.

As table 35 shows, Samuels relates each of the two categories described above—"horizontal" and "vertical"—to pluralism and corporatism. In order to broaden his theory to politics as a whole, he adds "political integration" to the column containing intergovernmental and extragovernmental relations. Samuels concludes, however, that Japanese central-local relations cannot be labeled either pluralist or corporatist but are a mixture of elements of both. He cannot avoid this conclusion because both pluralist and corporatist theory, but especially the latter, are not yet clear or powerful enough to be reliable approaches to the study of Japanese politics and administration.

In a slightly different way, I would summarize my understanding of the terms as follows: pluralism is a political process in which various groups in society are conscious of their own interests and use representatives to elevate these interests into state policies valid for society as a whole; corporatism is a political process in which the state (specifically, the bureaucracy) uses its command of the powerful groups in society to determine from above the benefits for the various groups in society. In terms of these two categories, in the past local government in Japan was seen as corporatist. But if we look at two groups, the National Association of Governors and the National Association of City Mayors, which have become the foci of attention in terms of problems in the context of central-local relations, we may say—albeit inconclusively, because there is almost no careful analysis of their recent activities (see Ari 1960, for their activities at that time)—that they, as a whole, have become representatives of local interests. In this regard, they seem to have the same characteristics as locally elected Diet members, who mediate with the national government on behalf of local interests. But the Diet members mediate the interests of individual localities, while the two associations represent the interests of the prefectures and municipalities as a whole. It is natural, therefore, that the lobbying activities of each takes a different form.

It is not clear whether, if we limit our discussion of corporatism to the field of central-local relations, it is really appropriate to characterize it as directly opposed to pluralism. There are certainly times when coalitions of local groups such as the National Association of Governors and the National Association of City Mayors intervene among local governments on behalf of central interests. Perhaps, as many theorists have indicated, the constraint and guidance that Japan's central ministries and agencies impose on local governments are fairly substantial. We must recognize them as elements that support corporatism and the vertical administrative control model. But I have also noted that the same systems and procedures provide localities with access to the center and stimulate lobbying activities, making the state susceptible to the influence of local demands. Although postwar central-local relations continue to contain elements of corporatism, we can see a gradual expansion of pluralist elements. But before we can firmly reach this conclusion, the concept of corporatism must be clarified; at the same time, more attention is needed to the development of the various policy networks that cover the length and breadth of the state and society.

Finally, I would like to stress that these kinds of theories are meaningless unless they are based on some empirical evidence. There is a danger that debates divorced from empirical data will degenerate into sterile ideological disputes. Indeed, my own discussion has frequently ended with merely hypothetical assertions.

Unlike previous discussions, my discussion of central-local relations in this book does not confine itself to the sphere of administration; rather, it tries to push into the world of politics. I would like to take up several points here that I feel deserve discussion. First, we need not think that centralization and autonomy exist in a zero sum relationship, or that they are mutually exclusive. Assuming mutual exclusiveness bespeaks an overly legalistic understanding. Reality includes the political potential for using the centralized system autonomously.

Second, local governments are able to demonstrate their autonomy because they have previously little-noted political resources. Among these is the phenomenon of state dependence on local government, which has arisen because most of the programs of the welfare state rely on local governments for implementation. Moreover, the very fact that more and more local programs entail dependence on the state has stimulated local governments to use their influence on the center. The locally elected national politicians' potential for exercising influence on the center is also great. Thus, studies of central-local relations cannot be limited to questions of legal interpretation but must become broadly comparative, or—if domestic—they must analyze specific policies; then for the first time this subject area will become of broader interest for students of political science and public administration.

Third, when local government expands in importance as part of the whole political process, as at present, to discuss the basic characteristics of local government is to discuss the basic characteristics of the political process or the political system. Conversely, in discussing the political process or the political system, we cannot omit the analysis of local politics. That comparative political scientists have focused more and more on the subject of local politics is for exactly this reason.

CHAPTER 6

The Overlapping Authority
Model of Central-Local
Relations

Throughout this book, I have stressed the need to consider local government within the context of the political process and
then, focusing on the overlapping authority model of Japanese intergovernmental relations and its horizontal political competition submodel, I have attempted to provide specific content for them. But this
model and submodel are derived mainly from observations of local government in the 1960s and 1970s. To what extent are they appropriate for
the period beginning in the 1980s?

The first half of the 1980s was an era of administrative and fiscal reform. The second half turned toward policies of expanding domestic
demand in response to international pressures. But already during the
last year of the Nakasone government, increasing revenues through tax
reform rather than decreasing expenditures had become a political
issue. Consequently central-local relations became rather different
from what they had been in the early 1980s. Specifically, the position
of local governments amid the process of reform became an important issue. Yet the orientation toward administrative and financial reform of the early period did not disappear; instead, it continued in the
form of private-sector scrutiny of the public sector. As international
pressures intensified, this scrutiny carried over into serious consideration of the implications of agricultural subsidies and protectionism.
What are the implications of this new process for the overlapping authority model?

Central-Local Relations
and the Reforms of the Early 1980s

Let us look at the kinds of themes that generated theories of central-local relations in the 1980s. The decade began with administrative and financial reform. During the Fukuda (1976–78) and Ōhira (1978–80) governments, the issue of the dramatically expanding deficit had already created a strong feeling that economizing reforms were necessary. But because of international pressures (the notion that a vigorous Japanese economy should serve as a "locomotive" for the international economy), Fukuda had not been able to tackle the issue, and Ōhira, who tried to resolve the problem by increasing revenues (with a tax hike), met with complete defeat in the 1979 general election. Against this background, when Prime Minister Suzuki took over the cabinet after Ōhira's death, he—in cooperation with Administrative Management Agency chief Nakasone—began to work for administrative and financial reform with the goal of reducing expenditures. The result was the establishment of the Second Provisional Administrative Reform Commission (Second Rinchō), with its slogan of "Financial reconstruction with no tax increase" and Dokō Toshio as its chair.

A factor analysis of the increases in various budget categories reveals some of the trends that necessitated the Second Rinchō. The data reveal a definite pattern in the expansion of national expenditures during the fifteen years preceding the Second Rinchō. Specifically, the provision of "semipublic" goods, primarily expenditures related to social welfare, drove the increased spending. Within this period, two years stand out: 1974 (the year of the oil crisis) and 1978 (the year when the "locomotive" argument in the summit talk drove expenditures up).

What I have said about expenditures applies not only to the national government but also, for the most part, to local governments. As local governments took charge of welfare and public works programs, the tendency described above seemed to become even stronger. In figure 5, which shows changes in the number of public officials since 1880, the differences in the implementation structures of national and local government become clear. Specifically, as a result of the Total Number of Civil Servants Law of 1968, the number of national public officials hardly increased at all after the mid-1960s. Because the central ministries and agencies could not increase their staffs, we can see a change in their methods of implementation. Thereafter, increased implementation of state policies

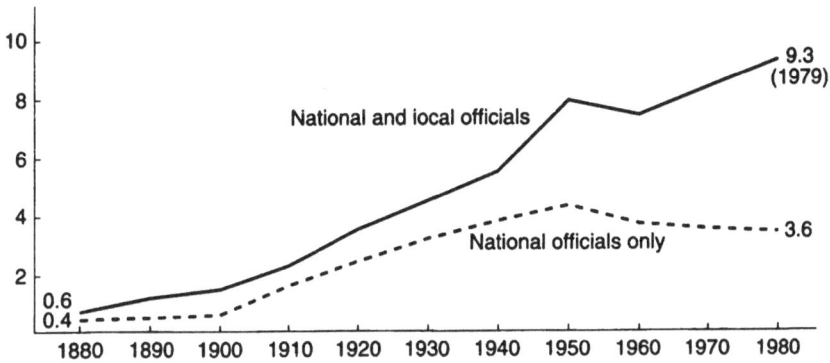

Figure 5. Percentage of Public Officials in the Working Population. *Source: Yano 1981.*

meant increased expenditures for contracted-out or subsidized work, which caused local governments to increase their expenditures and personnel. In the local governments, implementation and manpower have usually seemed to go together. The 1980s, in particular, brought a remarkable increase in personnel connected with the supervision of facilities and social welfare. Moreover, many programs have legally mandated numbers of staff. Also, with the proliferation of progressive local governments, there have been indications of increasing influence from public workers' unions and an easing of control of personnel size.

It is clear from its report that the Second Rinchō put local administrative and financial reform on the firing line. One of the council's four sections was devoted entirely to "national and local relations." In accord with the "Second General Outline of Administrative Reform" issued in 1985 by the Ministry of Home Affairs, based on the Second Rinchō report, the ministry called for the establishment of councils with the goal of political reform in every local (prefectural and municipal) government and requested reports on their findings. Seizing what they saw as a good opportunity, some local governments reorganized or abolished their personnel management systems and subsidized programs. But others created new organizations, and many made no more than *pro forma* studies in order to provide the Ministry of Home Affairs with the reports it demanded. In some localities, along with the establishment of the Second Rinchō, spontaneous financial reforms were introduced, as well as efforts at privatization in functional sections (for example, there were cases where preschools were transferred from public to private operation). The responses were myriad, varying with the local government.

The Second Rinchō and the Nakasone government saw local autonomy only in financial terms. But they also thought that the responsibility for reinvigorating the economy should be carried out by privatization through deregulation. Generally, after the Second Rinchō the following occurred in the operations of each ministry and agency: (1) budgetary and organizational downsizing based on overall ceilings, (2) privatization or private operation, (3) elimination of programs, and (4) the abolition or reduction of subsidies. A concrete example of administrative reforms can be seen in the cutting of "excess services"—such as the privatization of the Japan National Railroad (under the Ministry of Transport) and the Ministry of Health and Welfare's introduction of partial patient payment for medical care for the aged. In sum, reform sought to achieve "small government" through "deregulation" and "financial reconstruction without increased taxes," as the Second Rinchō itself indicated.

The Ministry of Home Affairs mediated relations with local governments in those matters in which the Second Rinchō and the prime minister were not directly involved. They carried out a campaign for greater efficiency and more economy, bringing staff levels and salaries, and even the size of local assemblies, under fire. There were also corresponding citizens' activities. Nishio Masaru and his group have called this intense pressure "neo-neo-centralization" (Nishio et al. 1983; Shindō 1986b). The thrust of their argument is that an intense new pressure was being applied by the center on local governments, but I would like to express subtle disagreement with at least two points. First, this pressure from the center has been for local governments *not* to do something, rather than for them to *do* something. The state is aiming for "small" rather than "big government." In this, the central government is saying that its previous control of local governments could be reduced. The reduction of subsidies since 1981 and the proposed revision (in 1987) of the Local Government Act to eliminate agency-delegated functions (albeit in combination with strengthened national proxy rights) both emerged from this context. Second, the pressure to transfer some operations and burdens to the private sector or households, which the Second Rinchō promoted, was welcomed by leaders of local government. Local governments were subject to considerable pressure from below—from citizens and organizations—to reduce their scale, as well as from the state and (in the case of municipalities) from the prefectures; moreover, they were largely receptive. Local governing bodies were liberated from the traditional control from above, and in order to restore their own autonomy and authority they had to think seriously about reducing their operations and slimming down. Trimming off the fat and focusing on truly essential administrative needs seems linked to a reinvigoration of the public sphere.

The 1980s and After

On the basis of the above, I would like to speculate about the future direction of central-local relations. To begin, I would like to take up some research data from the mid-1980s.

In order to examine the opinions of groups in the state bureaucracy, I will use survey data from a study I carried out in 1985–86. First, let us consider the responses, divided by ministry or agency, to the question "Do you think that your ministry (or agency) is going to have closer or looser relations with local governing bodies in the future?" (table 36). Fifty-two percent replied "much closer" or "somewhat closer." This response, which was higher than predicted, indicates that high-level bureaucrats anticipate that, even in an era of reform, the density of central-local relations in Japan is going to increase. With the next most frequent response, "the same as now," at 42 percent, most (94 percent) of the responses are accounted for. Responses of "looser" came almost entirely from the Ministry of Labor and Ministry of Health and Welfare, which have lost local administrative positions, and the Ministry of Finance, which is trying to cut back the budget. Rather than reforms "for the future," the respondents were thinking about real-life problems, such as the increase in older people.

What kind of content does a "closer" response have? We have no direct data on this, but responses to questions about whether local financial resources should be increased or not allow us to address the question. When we compare similar questions in a 1976 survey to the 1985–86 survey, we discover that the responses that local resources should be increased fell only from 40 percent to 39 percent. But responses that the situation was "sufficient at present" rose sharply from 36 percent to 46 percent. And those who responded that local resources were "already too large" increased from 4 percent to 13 percent. (For the first study see Muramatsu 1981b: chap. 7; for the second, see table 37.) It is interesting that while, according to table 36, central bureaucrats predict that relations with local governing bodies will become closer, they do not want

Table 36 *Relations between Ministries and Local Governing Bodies*

Ministry or Agency	Much Closer (%)	Somewhat Closer (%)	Same as Now (%)	Somewhat Looser (%)	Much Looser (%)	No Answer (%)	%	N
Economic Planning Agency	14	38	48	0	0	0	100	21
Ministry of Finance	2	24	61	7	0	5	100	41
Ministry of Health and Welfare	5	27	51	15	2	0	100	41
Ministry of Agriculture, Forestry, and Fisheries	18	35	41	6	0	0	100	34
Ministry of International Trade and Industry	28	60	13	0	0	0	100	40
Ministry of Labor	11	41	33	15	0	0	100	27
Ministry of Construction	29	39	32	0	0	0	100	31
Ministry of Home Affairs	13	31	56	0	0	0	100	16
Average	15	37	42	5	0	1	100	251

QUESTION: Do you think that your ministry (or agency) is going to have closer or looser relations with local governing bodies in the future?

Table 37 *Independent Local Financial Resources*

Ministry or Agency	Need Much More (%)	Sufficient at Present (%)	Too Large (%)	No Answer (%)	%	N
Economic Planning Agency	67	29	5	0	100	21
Ministry of Finance	12	46	37	5	100	41
Ministry of Health and Welfare	29	66	5	0	100	41
Ministry of Agriculture, Forestry, and Fisheries	32	53	12	3	100	34
Ministry of International Trade and Industry	38	43	15	5	100	40
Ministry of Labor	15	63	15	7	100	27
Ministry of Construction	16	71	13	0	100	31
Ministry of Home Affairs	100	0	0	0	100	16
Average	39	46	13	2	100	251

QUESTION: Which is closest to your opinion on the independent financial resources of local governing bodies?

to provide funds to strengthen local finances. How should we interpret this? I think it reflects the Second Rinchō and the Nakasone government of the 1980s, in two ways.

First, at a time when the growth of the budget was either zero or very low, the center feared that funds it could use would be stolen by the local governments. But the center also wanted the local governments to do its work. It thought that there were many functions that had to be implemented by using local governments as its partner.

Second, in the first survey there was a tendency to sanction the growth of local resources, which was most common in such "liberal" agencies as the Ministry of Home Affairs and the Economic Planning Agency, which tended to back local interests. If we look at the results of the survey according to ministry or agency, the responses are fairly harsh once we leave out the Ministry of Home Affairs, which strongly insisted on an increase in local resources. In the Ministry of Finance, 37 percent said that resources were "too large." When we add "sufficient at present" (46 percent), the overall pattern is hardly generous (see table 37). In comparison, agencies concerned with local programs responded at least "sufficient at present" and seemed to stress that resources should increase if possible. Therefore, if we look for a trend, a picture emerges of the Ministry of Finance versus the other ministries. Within "the other ministries," it is the Ministry of Home Affairs that most emphasizes enriching local resources.

Next, let us look at the attitudes and opinions of local officials, as shown in tables 38 and 39. The data were drawn from a Japan Urban Center study conducted in 1986 (Nihon Toshi Sentā 1986). When we use them to compare local officials' evaluation of the state and central officials' evaluation of local governments, the center's criticism of local government is more severe. While 43 percent of the municipal bureaucrats evaluated the central government as "well managed," only 39 percent of the state bureaucrats responded that the local level of government was "well managed." In the self-evaluations of central and local officials, the former were overwhelmingly positive (67 percent and 48 percent said "well managed"). The central government was not evaluated by local officials as highly as central officials evaluated themselves, but the degree of criticism it received from local officials was lower than the degree of criticism that local governments received from the center. On the basis of these data, is it likely that central-local relations will change along the lines of demands by the center for local improvement and change.

Table 38 *Management of the Central Administration*

Official	Managed Very Well (%)	Managed Some-what Well (%)	Not Managed Very Well (%)	Not Managed Well at All (%)	No Answer (%)	%	N
National	1.9	67.1	28.8	0	2.2	100	416
Prefectural	0.4	48.2	49.3	1.1	1.1	100	282
Municipal	0.6	41.9	55.8	1.2	0.6	100	339
Unidentified	0	71.4	28.6	0	0	100	7
Average	1.1	53.8	43.1	0.7	1.3	100	1,044

QUESTION: How do you regard the management of today's central administration?
SOURCE: Nihon Toshi Sentā 1986: 220.

Table 39 *Management of Local Administrations*

Official	Managed Very Well (%)	Managed Some-what Well (%)	Not Managed Very Well (%)	Not Managed Well at All (%)	No Answer (%)	N
National	0.2	38.9	53.1	4.1	3.6	416
Prefectural	0.4	51.4	45.4	1.1	1.8	282
Municipal	0	44.2	53.7	1.2	0.9	339
Unidentified	14.3	42.9	42.9	0	0	7
Average	0.3	44.1	51.1	2.3	2.2	1,044

QUESTION: How do you regard the management of today's local administrations?
SOURCE: Nihon Toshi Sentā 1986: 220.

If we combine the interpretations found in these two tables regarding the central bureaucracy, we see that the line ministries and agencies are not eager to give money to the local governments, but nevertheless they predict closer relations with local government. But because the center is critical of local government, we can surmise that in the future as well, it intends to make strong demands on them. There seems to be receptivity on the local side as well. Here the elements of vertical administrative control within the overlapping authority model come to the fore. In a sense, the center plans to push local governments back a little. This situation certainly does not augur well for the pursuit of local autonomy. But in the center's plans for "small government" and for increased domestic economic demand, there lies a chance for local governments to choose what is truly important to them. I will consider this point a little more in the next section.

The Concentration in Tokyo, Quality of Life, and an Aging Population

When we try to envision the course of the future, first we must see what form the administrative and financial reforms will settle into. During the time that I was writing this book, the Nakasone government, which carried out the reforms, fell. As of 1988, it seemed that the budget would increase somewhat under the new Takeshita cabinet, and the system of central-local relations might cause the horizontal competitive elements to expand again. Because any financial prediction involving the central-local relationship is related to the content and form of tax reform under debate (consumption tax), it is even more difficult to discuss now than previously.

What other kinds of issues will be important? One important factor for the future of Japanese local government is the extreme concentration of people, power, and wealth found in Tokyo.

The phenomenon of extreme concentration in Tokyo is above all an economic and social phenomenon that arose as a result of the operation of the free market. But it is also a political and administrative problem; indeed, the skyrocketing of land prices in the late 1980s was the greatest political problem of the Takeshita government.

There is no one cause for the phenomenon of Tokyo's overconcentration. Above all, as I noted above, it was brought about by the working of the Japanese market economy. In the background is the international-ization of the economy. And we can add cultural and political causes. Po-litical scientists and scholars of public administration pay attention to political causes, and some argue that Tokyo's position as the capital (the political and administrative center) is the greatest cause of its runaway expansion. I myself lean toward the market explanation, but even so we must not overlook the fact that the phenomenon of concentration in Tokyo is the reverse side of central-local relations.

The horizontal political competition model describes a situation in which local governments nationwide oppose one another, engaging in competition to acquire subsidies from "Tokyo"—that is, the central gov-ernment—in order to raise administrative standards. This phenomenon can be explained by the concept of administrative superiority found in the traditional vertical administrative control model, but I have argued that it is motivated by local elections. "Political" competition at the local level raises the position of locally elected Diet members in two ways and intertwines them with local politics. First, Diet members act as local agents to acquire what local governments want from the center. Second, they are not interested in causing decreases in the shared resources and means (authority, subsidies, personal networks) that make their role possible or even necessary. In this sense, they are also agents of the cen-tral government. The state's desire to participate in local affairs is shared not only by the central bureaucratic system of ministries and agencies, but by party politicians as well. The battle for shares within the center, which determines the overall framework of state resources for local in-tervention, is waged between politicians and bureaucrats.

In Tokyo there is no question that local pressure from the bottom up, through the political and administrative system, played a part in making the city central. The greater the number of matters that can be settled only by bargaining with the center—even if this is not by central fiat but ac-cording to the wishes of local governments—the more provincial actors make the trip to Tokyo. Every prefecture and big city has a branch office in Tokyo near the Diet building or the state ministries. And these pil-grimages to the capital encourage Tokyo-oriented behavior in enterprises all over the country. This set of political and administrative mechanisms nurtures a state of mind that inflates the political value of Tokyo. Even though local governments throughout Japan are carrying out their own wishes and decisions, their excessive competition is making Tokyo fat.

As I noted above, during the election process local public officials make promises to the citizens, which are carried all the way to the center because of competition within and between local governments. Because locally elected Diet members play a major role as agents in this process, the nature of reform concerning the redistribution of Diet seats is an important factor determining the character of central-local relations. Redistricting has reduced the number of members representing agricultural areas. As a result, local activity directed toward the center will probably decrease. If the governments of agricultural localities reduce their activity in this way, they have a chance to revive their "self-control," but do they have the resources to carry it through? If we see the concentration in Tokyo as a problem, we must also question the local will for autonomy as well as the allocation of resources. Fundamentally, the state determines the extent of local autonomy, but we must also pay attention to the posture of local governments themselves in determining their affairs.

Next, as we analyze local policy making, we must consider the quality of life that serves as the basic standard for policies. In the future, the concept of quality of life as the value underlying policies will become extremely important. In the past, Japan's political, economic, social, and administrative systems have all been biased toward economic development. Certainly since the emergence of pollution problems in the late 1960s, policies have become infused with environmental considerations in addition to their economic focus. Welfare issues have also gradually made themselves felt. And the fact that these new value premises were adopted in local policy making before they were adopted at the center confirms the major role of local government in Japanese policy formation. In addition, quality of life is conceptually important as a force, generated locally, that demands change in the central policy system—that is, the concept of quality of life implies both temporal and spatial policy themes.

For example, the completion of sewer systems is a continuation of modernization. So are urban parks. But the complete adoption of the two-day weekend, the availability of a highly developed transportation system, and other improvements in urban facilities will lead to a dramatic increase in the spatial scale of land use for leisure, recreation, culture, and residence. With any luck we will also see a rapid increase in public space. Then the themes of local government must change considerably, and quality of life issues will become more personal.

But given the present local power structure it is hard for quality of life concerns to become central issues. Even at the local level, the new middle class—which is sensitive to the quality of life—has little influence.

And as we see from the composition of local legislatures, the influence of old middle-class groups (farmers and self-employed people) in local politics is still unexpectedly strong. They are attached to the existing policy system. Most legislators come from agriculture, forestry, and fishing; small businesses; corporate leadership; and labor union leadership (Muramatsu and Itō 1986). Legislators from the first two general areas serve in addition to their regular jobs, while those from the latter two devote themselves exclusively to politics. But even those who continue to hold their regular jobs do so only for income, and in fact devote almost all their time to the job of legislator. In effect, their lifestyles give them the temporal flexibility needed to be local legislators. To amplify this point, people outside these occupational groups are handicapped in becoming legislators. The largest such group is salaried employees. Not only do very few become local legislators, but also they rarely join in petitioning or lobbying activity with regard to the making or implementation of everyday policy. Consequently, their views are rarely reflected in this policy. Only when employees become organized will they influence policy. We can point to the participation of two-job couples in demands for day nursery facilities, but so far such cases are rare.

As a result, some people argue that the only path to a high standard of living lies in international criticism of Japanese working hours and housing facilities. At the same time, there is a feeling that, because a number of new programs are already aiming at higher standards, the central and local governments may together be able to move toward the development of a better environment. But whether local society can generate from within the desire for higher standards of living depends on the middle class in urbanized areas. The question becomes: will the members of this class unite? Or, as somebody has suggested, will Japanese males continue to be workaholics and will it be their wives who advance the opinions and interests based on a concern for quality of life? Alternatively, as wives may share their values with their husbands, will direct alliances of working women come to demand a better quality of life? It seems clear that the future of local government depends on the division of labor and occupational cooperation between men and women. In any case, superseding all these questions is the question of the nature of "modernity," that is, the question of how modern man allocates his time between community and occupational or organizational activities.

Within the overlapping authority model, central-local relations of the future will change as the center of gravity moves first to the center and then returns to local government. The surplus functions of the horizontal political competition model, which invite new central pressure and lie behind Tokyo's extreme concentration, are not entirely positive. But the concept of quality of life brings their positive side to the fore again.

Finally, the emerging era of an aging population is too great a problem to fit neatly into the future of local government. I feel that given their great capacity for action, Japan's local governments have a great potential for coping with this era. But it will require fundamental reforms of the tax and financial system.

In concluding this chapter, I would like once more to place Japan's local government in a comparative perspective.

As part of the local reforms of 1986, British Prime Minister Margaret Thatcher abolished the Greater London Council (established in 1965) and various metropolitan authorities created in 1972–74. Most metropolis-wide programs were divided among the existing local governing bodies (districts and boroughs), while a few were entrusted to regional or joint boards. Some were also discarded as unnecessary. Most important, the administration abolished local governments' sole autonomous revenue source, the "rate" or property tax, and introduced a bill for a sort of head tax called the "community charge."

These British reforms seem to have been carried out efficiently. The same was true of the reforms of 1972–74—which, easily established by the will of Parliament, were equally easily undone under Thatcher. The power of the British Parliament is almighty. In Japan, unless plans for change are laid very cautiously, the prefectures and municipalities raise a great outcry all up and down the system; when this clamor collides with the central government head-on, it can put a stop to all local reform. And even if reform is handled skillfully, intense politicking and wheeling and dealing follow, centering on the restructuring of the various interests that the reform has created. After observing the British reforms, I really think that Japanese local government has become thoroughly rooted as the basic structure of Japanese politics. Indeed, in a sense its roots look stronger—or at least less vulnerable to facile change—than in England. But there is a problem here. When relations of overlapping authority put down deep roots, there is a danger that central-local relations will become immobilized. I think there is a need for a fundamental reexamination of the whole system of local government.

Epilogue

Toward a Larger Framework
for Local Government

Since I presented the conclusions of my discussion of local government in chapter 6, perhaps it is superfluous to add anything. But I would like to include here a few thoughts that I could not adequately discuss in the text of this book.

The focus of this book progressed from central-local relations to local government in general. The search for possibilities of autonomy in relations with the center is a commonplace in local government theory. But I have noted in this book that it is impossible in a country like Japan, where central and local government are closely intertwined, to construct a theory of local autonomy unless we reinterpret the meaning of autonomy in a contemporary context. This has been a stumbling block for many scholars of Japanese local government. When they look at the history of Japan before World War II, or even at the development of the more democratic postwar welfare state, Japanese scholars recognize the scope of the centralized system and how greatly it has expanded, and they conclude that there can be no independent local government in Japan. But there is a problem in this line of thinking, because their concept of local government is mainly a legalistic one.

In contrast, my conclusion—from a more political standpoint—is that local governments do possess independent wills and independent policies. To the extent that local governments enjoy the support of their citizens, central-local relations—in which the three levels of government have a complex system of shared powers and activities—are not impossible in Japan. Nevertheless, as many have pointed out, central control and supervision restrict local government. Examples of the "centralized system" at work are the center's pressure on local governments to reduce expenditures after the Second Rinchō and its strategy of shifting the burden for central expenses onto the shoulders of local governments. But in spite of these realities, the overlapping network of central-local authority opens windows for local government ingenuity; as I have strongly argued in this book, what moves the network from below is the internal politics and decision processes of local government.

Moreover, the fact-finding committees of local assemblies and newspaper surveys in every locality suggest that the internal processes of local government are becoming pluralistic. In the city of Kyoto, for example, the authority that the mayor thought he could continue to exercise unilaterally in his relations with the center (during the Takayama administration) was divided up early in 1970 under the Tomii and Funabashi administrations in Kyoto. We can no longer predict simply by looking at the mayor and the administration what policies will be produced.

Finally, I wish to relate the impressions I developed about Japan's local government and central-local relations as I wrote this book. I offer these to the reader not as analysis but simply as my impressions.

In this book I have presented a theory of local government that differs from earlier ones, and I have evaluated the various systems and methods that control contemporary Japanese local government—yet we cannot stop there. Local government can influence the center, but from a broader perspective the question arises whether this is desirable. The state tries to influence local government because the state is involved in the business of local governments through the sharing of functions. As a result, there is a danger that the center will waste its time and energy with a lot of unnecessary affairs. Both the state and the local governments tend to undermine the usefulness of the local government system, which could carry out many important tasks that the two levels of government each tend to see as distinctively their own.

When the center and local governments do take steps together under the present system, it is possible for them to put projects into practice efficiently, if often uniformly. This has the merit of accomplishing the center's goals swiftly. However, the problem is a resultant loss of both central and local energy, as seen in the complicated application for seeking subsidies. In a search of a new model, we may especially admire the autonomy of the large cities. Reforms that create large-scale local governments through consolidation or merger would liberate the prefectures; as a result, the form of local government at this prefectural level would gradually become a question of scope, jurisdiction, and character.

Now, let me broaden my perspective and say a few words about local autonomy and the entire present-day political structure of Japan.

We live in a period when the various functional relationships concerned with production and distribution are being restructured. This phenomenon can be seen in the extreme concentration of social, economic, and political functions in Tokyo. The reason so many company headquarters have moved to Tokyo is because a great many people and enterprises see Tokyo as the center of politics and administration. The metropolis of Tokyo is generally seen as the arena for state mediation of the main functional benefits of society, a view with which I concur. But we have not verified once and for all that this is a state-guided, corporatist relationship. I myself think that although the internationalization of economic and social activities and the enlargement of the state government functions that mediate between the expanded international system and the internal system have caused functional activities to accumulate in Tokyo, the primary propelling force that guides these activities is found among the actors of the international system and the actors of the internal private sector; the central government has been passive.

The integration of the international and internal systems has developed gradually, beginning with the postwar period; we must also recognize that the magnitude of the state's role has varied through time. In the period when Japan was seen as a "late-developing country," the leadership of the internal state-based system was much stronger than it is now; today, in a period controlled by the logic of a "borderless economy," the state has become relatively passive. But its mediating functions have expanded.

It is interesting that as the mediating activities of the state have expanded, the role of local governments seems to have expanded as well. In the 1930s, 1940s, and 1950s, the expansion of centrally subsidized projects seemed to attest to centralization in every sphere, but this point of view has since changed. In welfare policy as well, demands for standardized implementation were once thought to ensure centralization. However, as I and others have observed, welfarism in fact brought about a reliance of the center on local government and provided local governments with a chance to enhance their autonomy. This development has led to a reinvestigation of theories concerning central-local relations. In a discussion of public officials and administrators in a transitional period, Matsushita Keiichi said:

I think that big government is not inevitable; rather, it is a transitional phenomenon. The reason is because, in cultural and world history, the period from the nineteenth century until today has been an era of change from agricultural to urban society. In this process, not only did guarantees of high wages—rightly intended to solve classical poverty—become the order of the day, but so too did social security: the provision of social capital centered on urban problems and of social health, which grapples with pollution problems. But when each of these is fulfilled, doesn't the expansion of government also reach an optimum point? I think we can say that, because we are in an era of excess [demands for political benefits], we get big government and too many financial burdens. As urban society matures, won't it need less money once social security has been achieved, necessary social capital is in place, and pollution is adequately prevented? [Matsushita and Nishio 1979]

In response, Nishio Masaru suggested that there were places, however, where financial management was as necessary as it always had been:

I don't mean in the sense of taking the road that the advanced nations of western Europe have traveled. . . . Japan has never been as high as those advanced nations in its public expenditures in proportion to the GNP or in the number of public officials in national and local government in proportion to its working population. . . . Judging from this fact and from the necessity for preserving social capital and maintaining social security, we should expect that our country's expenditures and number of public officials will continue to increase. To expect them to stop at the present rate is an unrealistic fantasy. I think the question is rather how to generate some resistance to this growth and how to limit it in some way. [Matsushita and Nishio 1979]

Although these two speakers took different directions, both expressed views of the problems of government scale related to the basic framework of future central-local relations. What is especially interesting is that they agreed in distinguishing between "government" and "the public" and in not supporting the position that all public business should be carried out by the government. I too am interested in what kinds of organization may appear outside the government to assume public responsibilities. I expect that there will be an increase in organizations with real substance that are outside the public-private nucleus of the past—in such forms as so-called third-sector organizations (such as nongovernmental organizations, or NGOs), foundations, and volunteers.

Theoretically, there is a problem of representation. At an international conference on local government held in Turin (see Ōmori and Satō 1986), Sidney Tarrow argued that, even if an expansion of participation in policy making brings about a temporary concentration of policy-making functions, and even if it somewhat reduces the legislatures' power to make policy, it will not bring about a reduction in the importance of the representational function. Tarrow also noted that the representational axis was moving from the legislature to local government units or to individual members of the national legislative body. He based his observation on the increase in the frequency with which central government policies were executed by local governments. In this sense, even if the functional benefits of Tokyo's concentration are a centralization of all political, economic, social, and administrative functions, perhaps they are compensated for in part by the move of the representational axis to the local arena. The localities' concern is for policies of redistribution, especially in the form of subsidies. Even when they participate in economic policy, the localities focus their attention on redistribution, as they did during the period of local development in the late 1950s and early 1960s.

With the centralization of functional policy making and, perhaps, with a gain in the importance of international processes, the geographical locus of functional interests is found in Tokyo. But the locus of effective representation is moving to the local governments. I have described this change in Japan, but this view should be expanded to the comparative level.

Bibliography

Japanese-Language Sources

Abe Hitoshi. 1973. *Demokurashī no ronri*. Chūkō Shinsho.

Adachi Tadao. 1975. *Gyōsei to heikinteki shimin—tochi shūyō to shimin*. Nihon Hyōronsha.

——. 1978a. *Gendai no kōkyō mondai to shimin—heikinteki shimin no seijiteki seijuku*. Gyōsei.

——. 1978b. *Shokugyō to shite no kōmuin*. Kōmu shokuin Kenshū Kyōkai.

——, ed. 1975. *Gendai seiji to chihō jichi*. Yūshindō.

Akagi Suruki. 1978. *Gyōsei sekinin no kenkyū*. Iwanami Shoten.

Akimoto Ritsuo. 1971. *Gendai toshi no kenryoku kōzō*. Aoki Shoten.

Amakawa Akira. 1979. "Chihō jichihō no kōzō." In Nakamura Takafusa, ed., *Senryōki Nihon no keizai to seiji*. Tōkyō Daigaku Shuppankai.

——. 1983. "Kōiki gyōsei to chihō bunken." *Gyōsei no tenkanki* (special issue of *Jyuristo*).

Ari Bakuji. 1960. "Chihō rokudantai—chihō jichi o meguru zenkoku soshiki." In Nihon Seijigakkai, ed., *Nenpō seijigaku 1960-nen—Nihon no atsuryoku dantai*. Iwanami Shoten.

Ari Bakuji et al., eds. 1974. *Gendai seiji to kanryōsei*. 2 vols. Tōkyō Daigaku Shuppankai.

Ariizumi Sadao. 1980. *Meiji seiji shi no kiso katei—chihō seiji jōkyō shiron*. Yoshikawa Kōbunkan.

Asahi Jyānaru Henshūbu. 1969. *Machi no seiji mura no seiji*. Keisō Shobō.

Asukata Ichio. 1965. *Jichitai kaikaku no rirontaki tenbō*. Nihon Hyōronsha.

Chihō Gyōsei Chōsa Iinkaigi. 1950. *Gyōsei jimu saihaibun ni kansuru kankoku*, December 22.

Chihō Gyōsei Sōgō Kenkyū Sentā. 1974. *Jinkō kyūzō toshi no gyōzaisei mondai ni tsuite no chōsa kenkyū hōkokusho*.

———. 1981. *Atarashii shakai keizai jijō ni sokuō shita kokko hojokin no arikata ni tsuite.*

Daitoshi Seido Rekishi Hensan Iinkai. 1984. *Daitoshi seido shi.* Gyōsei.

Fujita Shōzō. 1966. *Tennōsei kokka no shihai genri.* Miraisha.

Fukutake Tadashi. 1965. *Chiiki kaihatsu no kōsō to genjitsu,* vols. 1–3. Tōkyō Daigaku Shuppankai.

Funaba Masatomi. 1986. *Kankyō no sentaku—jumin no motomeru kankyō asesumento.* Nihon Hyōronsha.

Furuki Toshiaki. 1977. *Chihō seiji no shakaigaku—kaikyūsei to kōkyōsei no ronri.* Tōkyō Daigaku Shuppankai.

Gendai Keizai Kenkyūkai, ed. 1974. *Kikan gendai keizai,* vol. 3, no. 15. Nihon Keizai Shinbunsha.

Gotō Ichirō, ed. 1977. *Kakkoku no chihō seido.* Kyōbundō.

Gyōsei Kanri Kenkyū Sentā. 1980. *1980 nendai ikō no gyōsei bijon ni kansuru chōsa kenkyū hōkokusho.*

———. 1985. *Seisaku jisshi katei ni okeru futan to kan'yo no arikata ni kansuru chōsa kenkyū kekka hōkokusho.*

Hirose Michisada. 1981. *Hojokin to seikentō.* Asahi Shinbunsha.

Ide Yoshinori. 1972. *Chihō jichi no seijigaku.* Tōkyō Daigaku Shuppankai.

Imamura Naromi. 1978. *Hojokin to nōgyō-nōson.* Ie no Hikari Kyōkai.

Inoguchi Takashi. 1983. *Gendai Nihon seiji keizai no kōzu—seiji to sijō.* Tōyō Keizai Shinpōsha.

Inuta Mitsuru and Hasegawa Fumio. 1981. *Chiiki "funsō" no kenkyū—jichitai no yakuwari to Gōi keisei no jōken.* Gakuyō Shobō.

Ishida Takeshi. 1956. *Kindai Nihon seiji kōzō no kenkyū.* Miraisha.

———. 1960. "Waga kuni ni okeru atsuryoku dantai hassei no rekishiteki jōken to sono tokushitsu." In *Nenpō seijigaku 1960-nen—Nihon no atsuryoku dantai.* Iwanami Shoten.

Isomura Eiichi and Hoshino Mitsuo, eds. 1957. *Chihō jichi tokuhon.* Tōyō Keizai Shinpōsha.

Isomura Eiichi, Ukai Nobushige, and Kawano Shigeto. 1971. *Toshi keisei no ronri to jumin.* Tōkyō Daigaku Shuppankai.

Iwai Tomoaki. 1981. "Kokkai ni okeru rippō kōdō no keiryōteki bunseki, 1965–1981." In Nakamura Akira and Takeshita Yuzuru, eds., *Nihon no seisaku katei.* Azusa-shuppan.

Iwasaki Mikiko. 1985. *Kanada renpōsei no seiji bunseki—renpō hojokin o meguru shomondai.* Ochanomizu Shobō.

Kanbara Masaru. 1986. *Tenkanki no seiji katei—rinchō no kiseki to sono kinō.* Sōgō Rōdō Kenkyūjo.

Kaneko Hitoshi. 1985. *Chihō jichihō.* Iwanami Shinsho.

Kansai Daigaku Keizai Seiji Kenkyōjo. 1982–84. *Toshi giin no taido to kōdō.*

Kataoka Hiromitsu. 1985. *Kuni to chihō—seifukan kankei no kokusai hikaku.* Waseda Daigaku Shuppanbu.

Katō Kazuaki. 1980. *Nihon no gyōzaisei kōzō.* Tōkyō Daigaku Shuppankai.

———. 1981. "Tokubetsu shisei mondai ni tsuite." In Toshi Mondai Kenkyūkai, ed., *Toshi gyōzaisei no kenkyū.* Ōsaka Shi Kenkyūjo.

———. 1986. "Bunken shōkai: M. Parkinson cho *Hinshi no ribāpūru*." *Hō to seiji*, vol. 37, no. 3.

Katō Tomiko. 1985. *Toshi keiei jichi e no tenkan—seisaki keisei to jumin sanka no shinhōkō*. Gyosei.

Katō Yoshitarō. 1982. *Jichitai no yosan kaikaku*. Tōkyō Daigaku Shuppankai.

Kawanaka Nikō. 1967. "'Chiiki seisaku' to chihō gyōsei." In Seijigaku Nenpō, *Gendai Nihon no seitō to kanryō*. Iwanami Shoten.

Kikan Gendai Keizai (Quarterly Journal of Contemporary Economics). (1974). Vol. 3, no. 15.

Kikegawa Hiroshi. 1955. *Meiji chihō seido no seiritsu katei*. Tōkyō Shisei Chōsakai.

Kita Nihon Shinbun Chihō Jichi Shuzaihan. 1970. *Yomigaere chihō jichi*. Keisō Shobō.

Kojima Akira. 1984. *Jichitai no yosan hensei—sono shiminka to kasseika*. Gakuyō Shobō.

Kume Ikuo. 1984. "Soshikinai kai tan'i no eikyōryoku (1, 2)—soshiki seiji moderu kōchiku no tame ni." *Hōgaku ronsō*, vol. 25, no. 5.

Kuroda Nobuyuki. 1983. *Gendai Nihon no chihō seijika—chihō giin no haikei to kōdō*. Hōritsu Bunkasha.

Kuze Kimitake and Hamada Kazunari. 1973. *Chihō gikai*. Shinchihō Jichi Kōza, vol. 2. Dai-ichi Hōki Shuppan.

Kyōdō Tsūshinsha. 1982. *Gyōsei kaikaku—chihō sentaku*. Dai-ichi Hōki Shuppan.

Masago Taisuke. 1975. "Chihō kōkyō dantai ni okeru gyōsei chidō—takuchi kaihatsu shidō yōkō o chūshin ni shite." In Adachi Tadao, Katō Kazuaki, Fukushima Tokujurō, Fukui Haruo, and Muramatsu Michio, eds., *Gendai seiji to chihō jichi*. Yūshindō.

Masumi Junnosuke. 1969. *Gendai Nihon no seiji taisei*. Iwanami Shoten.

Matsushita Keiichi. 1961. "Chiiki minshushugi no katei." *Shisō*, May.

———. 1971. *Shibiru-Minimamu no shisō*. Tōkyō Daigaku Shuppankai.

———, ed. 1971. *Shimin sanka*. Tōyō Keizai Shinpōsha.

Matsushita Keiichi and Nishio Masaru. 1979. "Conversation: Tenkanki no gyōsei to kōmuin." *Nihon no kōmuin* (Hōgaku Seminā special edition). Nihon Hyōronsha.

Mikuriya Takashi. 1986. "Suishigen kaihatsu to sengo seisaku kettei katei." In *Kanryōsei no keisei to tenkai*. Nihon kindai kenkyū, vol. 8. Yamakawa Shuppansha.

Mitani Taiichirō. 1967. *Nihon seitō seiji no keisei—Hara Takashi no seiji shidō no tenkai*. Tōkyō Daigaku Shuppankai.

Miyake Ichiro, Fukushima Tokujurō, and Muramatsu Michio. 1978. *Toshi seijika no kōdō to iken*. Kyōto Daigaku Jinbun Kagaku Kenkyūjo.

Miyake Ichiro and Muramatsu Michio. 1981. *Kyōto shi seiji no dōtai—daitoshi seiji no sōgōteki bunseki*. Yūhikaku.

Miyake Ichiro, Yamaguchi Yasushi, Muramatsu Michio, and Shindō Eiichi. 1985. *Nihon seiji no zahyō—sengo 40-nen no ayumi*. Yūhikaku.

Miyazawa Toshiyoshi. 1943. *Koyū jimu to inin jimu no riron*. Yūhikaku.

———. 1977. *Zaisei kaikaku—seikatsuken to jichiken no zaiseigaku*. Iwanami Shoten.

Miyoshi Shigeo. 1957. "'Chihō' an shūchō no riyū." *Jichi jihō*, December.

Mizuguchi Norihito. 1984. *Gendai toshi no gyōsei to seiji*. Hōritsu Bunkasha.

Murakami Hiroshi. 1983. "Nishi Doitsu ni okeru chūō chihō kankei no ichi danmen—inin jumu seido no chūshin ni, 1–4." *Jichi kenkyū*, vol. 59, nos. 1–8. Ryōsho Fukyūsha.

Murakami Yasasuke. 1985. *Shinchūkan taishū no jidai*. Chūōkōronsha.

Muramatsu Michio. 1969–70. "Amerika ni okeru daitoshiken kōiki seifu no keisei, 1, 2, 3." *Hōgaku ronsō*, vol. 84, no. 5; vol. 85, no. 3; vol. 87, no. 5.

———. 1971. "Chiiki shakai to funsō." *Hōgaku ronsō*, vol. 90, nos. 1–3.

———. 1975a. "Chihō seiji to shimin ishiki." In Kawano Kenji, ed., *Chiiki shakai no henbō to jumin ishiki*. Nihon Hyōronsha.

———. 1975b. "Gyosei katei to Seiji sanka." In Nihon Seijigakki, ed. *Seiji Sanka no riron to genjitsu*. Nenpō Seijigaku.

———. 1975c. "Sengo Nihon ni okeru chihō seiji." In Adachi Tadao, Katō Kazuaki, Fukushima Tokujurō, Fukui Haruo, and Muramatsu Michio, eds., *Gendai seiji to chihō jichi*. Yūshindo.

———. 1979a. "Chihō jichi ni okeru niritsu haihan—jiritsusei to gyōsei suijun (matawa katsudōryō) no torēdo-ofu." In Okazaki Chōichirō, Katō Kazuaki, Fukui Haruo, and Kamo Toshio, eds., *Chihō jichitai no genjō to kadai*. Gyōsei.

———. 1979b. "Chihō jichi riron no mō hitotsu no kanōsei." *Jichi kenkyū*, vol. 55, no. 7. Ryōsho Fukyūsha.

———. 1981a. "Hojokin seido no seiji byōseijō no igi." *Jichi kenkyū*, vol. 57, no. 9.

———. 1981b. *Sengo Nihon no Kanryōsei*. Tōyō Keizai Shinpōsha.

———. 1983a. "Chūō chihō kankeiron no tenkan—chūkan dantai to shite no fuken o chūshin ni." *Jichi kenkyū*, vol. 59, nos. 3–4.

———. 1983b. "Dai-ni rinchō tōshin o saiten suru." *Chūō kōron*, June.

———. 1984. "Chūō chihō kankei ni kansuru shinriron no mosaku—suiheiteki seiji kyōsō moderu ni tsuite." *Jichi kenkyū*, vol. 60, nos. 1–2.

———. 1985. "Shūkenka no moto ni okeru jichi gainen no saikentou—seiji kateiron no naka no chihō jichi." *Jichi kenkyū*, vol. 61, no. 1.

———. 1986. "Seifukan kankei to seiji taisei." In Ōmori Wataru and Satō Seizaburō, eds., *Nihon no chihō seifu*. Tōkyō Daigaku Shuppankai.

Muramatsu Michio and Itō Mitsutoshi. 1986. *Chihō giin no kenkyū*. Nihon Keizai Shinbunsha.

Nagahama Masatoshi. 1946. *Chiji kōsen no shomondai*. Yūhikaku.

———. 1950. *Kindai Kokkaron*, Part 2: *Kiō—kokka kinō no bunka to shūchū*. Kōbundō.

———. 1952. *Chihō jichi*. Iwanami Shoten.

Nakano Minoru, ed. 1986. *Nihongata Seisaku Keisei Katei no Henyō*. Tōyō Keizai Shinpōsha.

Narita Yorihiro. 1965. "Chihō jichi no hōgai." *Nihonkoku kenpō taikei*, vol. 5. Yūhikaku.

Narumi [Masayasu]. 1982. *Sengo jichitai kaikaku shi*. Nihon Hyōronsha.

Nihon Seijigakkai. 1967. *Gendai Nihon no seitō to kanryō—hoshu gōdōigo*. Seijikaku Nenpō.

———. 1985. *Kindai Nihon seiji ni okeru chūō to chihō.* Nenpō Seijigaku, 1984. Iwanami Shoten.

Nihon Toshi Sentā. 1986. *Chihō: Kokka kanbu kōmuin ishiki chōsa.*

Nishio Masaru. 1975a. "Jichi." In Nenpō Seijigaku, *Seijigaku no kiso gainen.* Iwanami Shoten.

———. 1975b. *Kenryoku to sanka—gendai Amerika no toshi gyōsei.* Tōkyō Daigaku Shuppankai.

———. 1979. "Kaso to Kamitsu no seiji gyōsei." In Nenpō Seijigaku, *55-nen taisei no keisei to hōkai.* Iwanami Shoten.

———. 1986. *Igirisu chihō jichi jijō.* Chihō Jichi Sōgō Kenkyūjo.

Nishio Masaru et al. 1983. "Sin-shin chuūō shūken to joichitai sentaku." *Sekai,* vol. 451 (June).

Ōhara Mitsunori and Yokoyama Keiji. 1965. *Sangyō shakai to seiji katei.* Nihon Hyōronsha.

Okayama Daigaku Chihō Jichi Kenkyūkai. 1985. *Shichōson gikai giin chōsa hōkoku—Okayama to Shinagawa no hikaku.*

Okazaki Chōichirō. 1981. "Tokubetsu shisei no undō to seidoka." In Toshi Mondai Kenkyūkai, ed., *Toshi gyōzaisei no kenkyū.* Ōsaka Shi Kenkyūjo.

Okazaki Chōichirō and Takagi Shōsaku. 1959. "'Chihō'-sei no kuiki to soshiki (1)—Chihō seido chōsakai tōshin no hihan." *Ritsumeikan Hōgaku,* no. 28.

Okita Tetsuya. 1968. *Chihō jichi yōron.* Hyōronsha.

———. 1976. "Shūken to bunken." In Tsuji Kiyoaki, ed., *Gyōseigaku kōza 4: Gyō-sei to soshiki.* Tōkyō Daigaku Shuppankai.

Ōmori Wataru. 1974. "Gendai gyōsei ni okeru 'jumin sanka' no tenbō—1960 nendai Amerika ni okeru 'comyunitī katsudō jigyō' no dōnyū to hen'yō." In Ari Bakuji et al., eds., *Gendai gyōsei to kanryōsei,* vol. 1. Tōkyō Daigaku Shuppankai.

———. 1985. "Renpōsei kokka—'seifukan kankei' no tenkan." In Satō Seizaburō, ed., *Jiyū to tōgō.* Nihon Keizai Shunbunsha.

Ōmori Wataru and Satō Seizaburō, eds. 1986. *Nihon no chihō seifu.* Tōkyō Daigaku Shuppankai.

Ōshima Tarō. 1981. *Jichitai kakushin no tenbō.* Miraisha.

Ōtake Hideo. 1981. "Shohyō: Sengo Nihon no kanryōsei." *Economisto,* April 28. Mainichi Shinbunsha.

Rekidai Chiji Hensankai, ed. 1981. *Nihon no rekidai chiji,* vol. 1. Rekidai Chiji Hensankai.

Rōyama Masamichi. 1949. *Eikoku chihō gyōsei no kaikaku.* Kokushisha.

———. 1953. *Chihō seido no kaikaku.* Shakai Shichōsha.

Sankei Shinbun Chihō Jichi Shuzaihan. 1973. *Kakushin Jichitai.* Gakuyō Shobō.

Sasaki Nobuo. 1985. *Gendai toshi gyōsei no kōzu.* Gyōsei.

Satō Atsushi. 1963–64. "Shinsangyō toshi no rinen to genjitsu." *Hōgaku seminā,* December–April.

———. 1964. "Nihon kanryōsei no mondaiten." In Aoi Kazuo, ed., *Soshiki no shakaigaku.* Yūhikaku.

———. 1965. *Gendai no chihō seiji.* Nihon Hyōronsha.

———. 1967. *Nihon no chiiki kaihatsu.* Miraisha.

Satō Kōji and Kyōto Shi Shimin Ishiki Kenkyūkai. 1973. "Kyōto shi ni okeru shimin ishiki (6) — Kyōto shisei ni okeru kenryoku imēji." *Hōgaku ronso,* vol. 94, no. 1.

"Seifukan Kankei" Kenkyū Shūdan (Nishio et al.). 1984. "Shinshin chūō shūken to jichitai no sentaku." *Sekai,* June.

Shibata Mamoru. 1975. *Jichi no nagare no naka de — sengo chichōzei zaisei gaikō.* Gyōsei.

Shimin. 1971. Vol. 1.

Shindō Muneyuki. 1986a. *Amerika zaisei no paradaimu: seifukan kankei.* Shin'yōsha.

———. 1986b. *Gendai seiji to gyōsei kaikaku.* Iwanami Shoten.

Shinohara Hajime. 1971. *Gendai Nihon no bunka hen'yō.* Renga Shobō.

Tachibana Takashi. 1980. *Nōkyō.* Asahi Shinbunsha.

Takagi Shōsaku. 1973. *Jumin jichi no kenri.* Hōritsu Bunkasha.

———. 1974. "Chiji kōsensei to chūō tōsei." In Ari Bakuji et al., eds., *Gendai gyōsei to kanryōsei,* vol. 2. Tōkyō Daigaku Shuppankai.

———. 1976. "Nihon no chihō jichi." *Gyōseigaku kōza, 2: Gyōsei no rekishi.* Tōkyō Daigaku Shuppankai.

———. 1979. "Todōfuken no jimu." In Zenkoku Chijikai, ed., *Hendōki ni okeru todōfukensei.*

Takayose Shōzō. 1978. *Chihō zaisei no kaikaku.* Keisō Shobō.

Tanaka Jirō. 1949. *Gyōseihō no kihon genri.* Yūhikaku.

Tsuchiya Kiyoshi and Ōkita Saburō, eds. 1963. *Nihon no chiiki kaihatsu.* Daiyamondosha.

Tsuji Kiyoaki. 1969. *Shinpan: Nihon kanryōsei no kenkyū.* Tōkyō Daigaku Shuppankai.

———. 1976. *Nihon no shihō jichi.* Iwanami Shoten.

Tsuji Kiyoaki et al., eds. 1965. *Gendai gyōsei no riron to genjitsu.* Keisō Shobō.

Toki Hiroshi. 1983. *Gendai no toshi seiji — hikaku, jisshō kenkyū.* Nihon Hyōronsha.

Toshi Mondai Kenkyūkai. 1981. *Toshi gyōazisei no kenkyū.* Toshi Mondai Kenkyūkai.

Yano Kōta Kinenkai, ed. 1981. *Nihon kokusei zue.* Kokuseisha.

Yokoyama Keiji and Ōhara Mitsunori. 1966. *Gendai Nihon no chiiki seiji.* Sanjūichi Shobō.

Yonehara Junshichirō. 1977. *Chihō zaiseigaku.* Yūhikaku.

Yorimoto Katsumi. 1974. *Gomi sensō.* Nikkei Shinsho.

———. 1985. "Shikyoku kōzō ni yoru seijika — kakushin jichitai no deiremuma." In Ōmori Wataru and Satō Seizaburō, eds., *Nihon no chihō seifu.* Tōkyō Daigaku Shuppankai.

English- and French-Language Sources

Advisory Commission on Intergovernmental Relations (ACIR). 1964. *The Role of Equalization in Federal Grants.* January.

Alderfer, Harold F. 1964. *Local Government in Developing Countries.* New York: McGraw-Hill.

Amakawa, A. 1982. "Regionalism and Autonomy: The Continuing Debate in Japan." Paper presented at the Conference on Local Institutions in National Development: Strategies and Consequences of Local-National Linkage in the Industrial Democracies, March 15–19, Bellagio, Italy.

Apter, David. 1971. *Choice and Politics of Allocation*. New Haven: Yale University Press.

Aqua, Ronald. 1979. "Politics and Performance in Japanese Municipalities." Ph.D. diss., Cornell University.

Ashford, Douglas. 1982. *British Dogmatism and French Pragmatism: Central-Local Relations in the Welfare State*. London: Allen and Unwin.

——. 1986. "Memo to the Participants for the Final Conference on Central-Local Relationships in Implementation." Bellagio, Italy.

Becquart-Leclerc, Jeanne. 1987. "Paradoxes of Decentralization in France." Paper presented at a workshop on French local government, February 12, Tokyo.

Beer, Samuel. 1978. "Federalism, Nationalism, and Democracy in America." *American Political Science Review*, vol. 72.

——. 1979. "The Modernization of American Federalism." *Publius*, vol. 3, no. 2.

Clark, Terry, ed. 1972. *Comparative Community Politics*. New York: Halsted Press.

Dahl, R. 1957. "The Concept of Power." *Behavioral Science*, vol. 2.

——. 1961. *Who Governs?: Democracy and Power in the American City*. New Haven: Yale University Press.

——. 1966. *Democracy in the United States*. Chicago: Rand McNally.

Deutsch, K. 1966. *The Nerves of Government: Models of Political Communication and Control*. New York: Free Press.

Elazer, Daniel. 1965. "The Shaping of Intergovernmental Relations in the Twentieth Century." *Annals of the American Academy of Political and Social Science*, vol. 359.

Eldersveld, S. J. 1964. *Political Parties: A Behavioral Analysis*. Chicago: Rand McNally.

Gouldner, A. 1964. "The Norm of Reciprocity: A Preliminary Statement." *American Sociological Review*, vol. 25.

Grodzins, M. 1967. "The Federal System." In Aaron Wildavsky, ed., *American Federalism in Perspective*. Boston: Little, Brown.

Gyford, John, and Marie James. 1983. *National Parties and Local Politics*. London: Allen and Unwin.

Hanf, K., and F. Scharpf. 1978. *Interorganizational Policy Making: Limits to Coordination and Central Control*. London and Beverly Hills: Sage Publications.

Hunter, Floyd. 1953. *Community Power Structure*. Chapel Hill: University of North Carolina Press.

Kesselman, Mark, and Donald B. Rosenthal. 1974. "Local Power and Comparative Politics." Paper presented to the annual meeting of the American Political Science Association, September 5–9, Washington, D.C.

Kincade, John. 1984. "Toward the Third Century of American Federalism: New Dynamics and New Perspectives." *American Studies International*, vol. 22, no. 1.

Lagroye, J., and Vincent Wright. 1979. *Local Government in Britain and France: Problems and Prospects.* London: Allen and Unwin.

Lajoie, André. 1968. *Les structures administratives régionales.* Montreal: Presses de l'Université de Montreal.

Long, N. 1962. *The Polity.* Chicago: Rand McNally.

Lowi, Theodore. 1981. *The End of Liberalism.* New York: Norton.

Martin, Roscoe. 1965. *The Cities and the Federal System.* New York: Atherton.

McKean, Margaret. 1981. *Environmental Protest and Citizen Politics in Japan.* Berkeley, Los Angeles, and London: University of California Press.

Mill, J. S. 1919. *Representative Government.* People's Edition. London: Longman, Green.

Milnor, A. 1984. "Administrative Bargaining and Social Policy: New York State." Paper presented to Meeting on the Policy Implementation in Social Policies, at GRAL, a study group of the Centre National de la Recherche Scientifique (CNRS), Paris.

Muramatsu, Michio. 1986. "A Lateral Political Competition Model for Japanese Central-Local Relations." *Journal of Japanese Studies,* vol. 12, no. 2.

Muramatsu, Michio, and Ronald Aqua. 1980. "Japan Confronts Its Cities: Central-Local Relations in a Changing Political Contest." In Douglas Ashford, ed., *National Resources and Urban Policy.* New York and Toronto: Methuen.

Muramatsu, Michio, and Ellis Krauss. 1984. "Bureaucrats and Politicians in Policymaking: The Case of Japan. *American Political Science Review,* Spring.

———. 1987. " 'The Conservative Policy Line' and the Development of Patterned Pluralism in Postwar Japan." In Kozo Yamamura and Yasukichi Yasuba, eds., *The Political Economy of Japan,* vol. 1. Stanford: Stanford University Press.

Nathan, Richard P., et al. 1975. *Revenue-Sharing in Practice.* Washington, D.C.: Brookings Institution.

Peterson, Paul E. 1987. *City Limits.* Chicago: University of Chicago Press.

Pressman, J. L., and A. Wildavsky. 1973. *Implementation.* Berkeley: University of California Press.

Reed, Steven. 1979. "Local Policy Making in a Unitary State: The Case of Japanese Prefectures." Ph.D. diss., University of Michigan.

———. 1982. "Is Japanese Government Really Centralized?" *Journal of Japanese Studies,* October.

Rhodes, R. A. W. 1982. *Control and Power in Central-Local Government Relations.* Westmead: Gower.

Rose, Richard. 1984. "From Government at the Center to Nationwide Government." Center for the Study of Public Policy, University of Strathclyde, Scotland.

Salisbury, R. 1964. "Urban Politics: The New Convergence of Power." *Journal of Politics,* vol. 26.

Samuels, Richard. 1983. *The Politics of Regional Policy in Japan: Localities Incorporated?* Princeton: Princeton University Press.

Simcock, Bradford L. 1972. "Environmental Pollution and Citizens' Movements: The Social Sources and Significance of Antipollution Protest in Japan." *Area Development,* no. 5.

Steiner, Kurt. 1965. *Local Government in Japan*. Stanford: Stanford University Press.

Suleiman, E. 1978. *Elites in French Society: The Politics of Survival*. Princeton: Princeton University Press.

Tarrow, Sidney. 1977. *Between Center and Periphery*. New Haven: Yale University Press.

Tarrow, Sidney, et al., eds. 1978. *Territorial Politics in Industrial Nations*. New York: Praeger.

Thoenig, Jean-Claude. 1978. "State Bureaucracies and Local Government in France." In K. Hanf and F. Scharpf, eds., *Interorganizational Policy Making*. London and Beverly Hills: Sage Publications.

Tocqueville, Alexis de. 1958.[1835–40] *Democracy in America*. Trans. Phillips Bradley. New York: Vintage.

Waldo, D. 1948. *The Administrative State*. New York: Ronald Press.

White, L. D. 1938. *Introduction to the Study of Public Administration*. New York: Macmillan.

Wright, Deil. 1978. *Understanding Intergovernmental Relations*, 2d ed. Monterey, Cal.: Brooks/Cole.

Index

Compositor: Impressions Book and Journal Services, Inc.
Text: 10/13 Galliard
Display: Galliard

www.ingramcontent.com/pod-product-compliance
Lightning Source LLC
Chambersburg PA
CBHW031133270326
41929CB00011B/1614